INTRODUCTION TO LIVE SOUND

Roland Higham

ENTERTAINMENT TECHNOLOGY PRESS

Application & Techniques Series

For Arthur Boscow, my grandfather
who started me off playing with tape recorders
and Tim Foster and George Glossop,
who got me started me professionally

INTRODUCTION TO LIVE SOUND

by Roland Higham

Entertainment Technology Press

Introduction to live Sound

© Roland Higham

First published March 2015
Entertainment Technology Press Ltd
The Studio, High Green, Great Shelford, Cambridge CB22 5EG
Internet: www.etnow.com

ISBN 978 1 904031 79 6

A title within the
Entertainment Technology Press Application & Techniques Series
Series editor: John Offord

CODE / ILS002_03-15

CONTENTS

PREFACE

This book is intended for the newcomer and experienced engineer. I hope it will instruct the student and reaffirm some fundamental principles for the experienced engineer.

1 INTRODUCTION

There are many excellent technical books out there which describe in great mathematical detail as much as it is possible to describe, as long as you know enough to find the right page to start with; this is not one of those books. Instead it aims to provide working engineers and newcomers alike with a concise knowledge base that explains some of the theory and principles that they will encounter every day and to provide a little more insight into such things. It forms an introduction to many topics that will be covered in more detail in later books in the series. In addition it should provide the student and newcomer to the field a valuable compendium of helpful knowledge. By far the hardest part has been trying to decide what to leave out rather than what to include.

Sound engineering in all its forms can be a fun and rewarding vocation but it can also be stressful and pressured and like many professions sensitive handling of the human factors can often make the difference between success and failure; the better your knowledge and understanding of the technicalities, the better your ability to deal with the situations that arise and the more you can concentrate on the artistry and rewards and manage your client's expectations with care and realism.

A greater understanding of the underlying principles can only serve to simplify your endeavours – to help you achieve your goals more quickly and more effectively.

I have taken the approach of both ends towards the middle in the format of this book: that is I have tried to explain the background of acoustics and electronics, then moved on to explore how these principles apply to the selection and use of loudspeakers and microphones. Only then have I moved into the exclusively 'electronic' realm of the mixing console and ancillary equipment. My reason for this is simple – if you get the right loudspeakers in the right place and choose the right microphone for the job and get those in the right place, what you have to do with the mixing console should be the simplest part of the job.

2 WHAT IS SOUND?

Sound is a very powerful thing. We cannot simply shut it out as we can light by closing our eyes. It can grab our attention, it can take us to a high state of alert, it can sooth and calm us, it can communicate anything that language has the power to describe. As music it can carry emotions that are virtually impossible to achieve in other ways. All this is pretty impressive for a simple variation of air pressure!

Imagine a thing making a sound. It could be a loudspeaker cone or the soundboard of a string instrument or, as drawn below, the prongs of a tuning fork moving in and out. When moving outwards, the air in front is compressed, causing a region of high pressure to travel away, when moving inwards the air is decompressed, causing a region of low pressure to move away. These continuously oscillating pressure waves travel away from the source at a fixed speed that is independent of their frequency. This is sound – just a pressure wave propagating through the air in much the same way as ripples propagate away from a stone dropped into a pond. Of course sound can travel through any tangible medium such as air, water, concrete or steel and the nature of the medium dictates the way it travels. Since we have evolved as air-breathing land animals, I will consider the behaviour of sound in air as our medium in almost all cases.

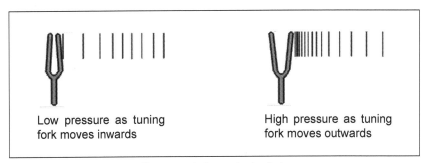

Low pressure as tuning fork moves inwards

High pressure as tuning fork moves outwards

Fig 2.1 Sound wave propagation example from a tuning fork.

When you hear sound, the variations in air pressure cause a membrane in your ear (the ear-drum or tympanic membrane) to oscillate in sympathy with the variation in air pressure. This in turn moves a 'mechanism' of three bones (called ossicles) which are connected to the ear drum (also called the tympanic membrane) and these bones transfer that vibration to a fluid filled channel. Muscles connected to the ossicles can adjust the sensitivity of the ear by varying the tension in the ear-drum and so provide a variable mechanical gain that amplifies the tiny vibrations of the ear drum over a very wide range of sound levels. Inside the fluid filled channel (called the cochlea) these amplified vibrations cause minute hairs to vibrate in sympathy. These hairs convert the vibrations in the fluid to nerve impulses which pass to the brain and are perceived as sound. The ear is a fantastically delicate and sensitive instrument and must be treated with great care and respect; it is quite easy to damage beyond repair by excessive exposure to high sound pressure.

If we allow the same pressure variations to impinge onto the diaphragm in a microphone, then a broadly similar (but much more simple) process results in the conversion of sound to electricity. Once in electrical form, these signals can easily be manipulated in all sorts of ways: we can amplify then (to make then bigger) we can send them over great distances much faster than sound travels through air, we can selectively amplify or attenuate some frequencies and not others and many other tricks that we will look at. And we can even store this in one of many forms for use later where later can be anything from fractions of a second to years.

Wavelength and Frequency

Like all physical phenomena sound waves have parameters that we use to measure and describe them. The three basic ones are speed, wavelength and frequency. These are related by the formula:

$$v = f\lambda$$

Where v is speed (metres per second), f is frequency (Hertz) and λ is wavelength (metres).

I make no apologies for throwing in some maths so early into what is intended to be a low-maths book but this is one of the three main principles that are worth expressing mathematically and keeping in your memory. If you prefer to remember it in words:

speed is equal to **frequency** multiplied by **wavelength**

It is often more helpful to rearrange this simple formula to derive wavelength:

$$\lambda = {}^v\!/_f$$

Or in other words:

wavelength is equal to **speed** divided by **frequency**

The units are metres (m) for wavelength, metres per second (m/s or ms^{-1}) for speed and hertz (Hz) for frequency.

Some texts (mainly older and American) may refer to feet in place of metres, but using SI (metric) units keeps the maths very simple – which is why most scientific communities only use SI units for all things. And Hertz maybe written as cycles per second though this is the same thing.

Speed of Sound

The speed of sound is fixed[1] by the nature of the medium through which the sound is travelling, the 'stiffness' of this medium being the most significant factor. For example, sound in dry air at 20°C travels at approximately 343m/s. In stiffer materials sound travels much faster – in steel, for example it is about 5,960 m/s but in iron, which is a similar density but softer, the speed is lower at about 5100 m/s.

Temperature has a big effect on the properties of gases such as air, so we see a variation of about 10% in 'habitable' air temperature ranges:

Temperature (°C)	Speed of sound (m/s)	Speed of sound (mph)
-10	324	725
10	337	754
20	343	767
30	349	781
40	355	794

Table 2.1 Speed of sound in air at various temperatures.

I'd hope nobody would be doing events in temperatures very far outside of this range!

Speed and Distance

There is a simple relationship between speed, distance and distance which applies to all things that move:

---

1 Actually there can be small variations in the speed of sound caused by (for example) very large magnitude (high level) sounds but in our cases all these effects can be ignored.

$$s = \frac{d}{t}$$ speed is s, distance is d and time is t

To put this into words, speed is equal to distance divided by time. If you think about it, this makes perfect sense as all units of speed are expressed as a distance unit per time, such as miles per hour, kilometres per hour, metres per second, etc. This can be rearranged to a more useful formula:

$$t = \frac{d}{s}$$

Or time taken to travel a distance is equal to that distance divided by the speed.

So a sound wave travelling at 343ms⁻¹ over a distance of 34m will take 34/343 ≈ 0.1 seconds.

As a rough rule of thumb this amounts to 1ms (0.001 seconds or 1 thousandth of a second) per foot or 3ms (0.003 seconds or 3 thousandths of a second) per metre. Obviously for long distances this rule of thumb becomes increasingly inaccurate and it is best to reach for the calculator on your phone.

Frequency

Frequency is simply the number of times per second the pressure variations complete a cycle – higher notes and sounds oscillate more quickly and have a higher frequency. Older texts refer to frequency in 'cycles per second'. This verbose but descriptive unit has been replaced with Hertz (Hz) – but it is the same thing:

1Hz = 1 cycle per second, 1000Hz = 1000 cycles per second etc.

Fig 2.2 shows the frequencies and wavelengths of notes C and A on a piano keyboard and a number of other common instruments and vocal ranges. Be aware that an actual 'note' on an real instrument is composed of lots of different but related frequencies at different levels called harmonics and the upper limits of notes are often defined by the instrument and by playing techniques. The relationship between the harmonics and the fundamental give each instrument its distinct sound. The fundamental is the 'root' or sound on which all others for that note are based and as such is always the lowest frequency present and the one which defines the pitch of that note.

You will notice that the frequency of each similar note (all the As for example) is exactly double or half the frequency of the one below or above it. For example:

A1 = 55Hz, A2 = 110Hz, A3 = 220Hz, A4 = 440Hz etc. This spacing

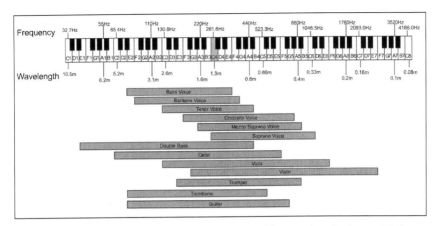

Fig 2.2 Comparison of various instruments' ranges and frequencies of notes and their wavelength.

(or interval) is referred to as an octave and is a doubling or halving of frequency.

In our modern musical world, each semitone interval, for example C to C# is related by a factor of $\sqrt[12]{2}$ (approximately 1.059). So if A1 = 55Hz then A1# (B1♭) = 55*1.059 = 58.27Hz. Don't worry, there's no reason to remember this; I just thought you might find it interesting. If you want to research the history of musical intervals, start by looking up equal temperament as described here.

So if we have a fixed speed of sound (for any given situation) and we know the frequency of a sound, then by using:

$$\lambda = {}^{v}\!/_{f} \text{ or wavelength } (\lambda) = \text{speed}(v) \div \text{frequency } (f)$$

And so we can work out the wavelength, as I have done in the fig 2.1.

Note	Frequency/Hz	Wavelength/m
A0 - 3 octaves below middle C	27.5	12.5
A1 - 2 octaves below middle C	55	6.2
A2 - 1 octave below middle C	110	3.1
A3 - below middle C	220	1.6
Middle C	261.3	1.3
A4 - above middle C	440	0.8

Note	Frequency/Hz	Wavelength/m
A5 - 1 octave above middle C	880	0.4
A6 - 2 octaves above middle C	1760	0.2
A7 - 3 octaves above middle C	3520	0.1

Table 2.2 Frequency of notes on the piano.

Our range of hearing is about 20Hz to 20,000Hz (20kHz[2]) which gives us a range of wavelength (in air at room temperature) of between 17.15m (20Hz) to 1.7cm (20kHz). This is a range of slightly less than 10 octaves: start with 20 and keep doubling until you get to 20,000 and you'll see that you can do this 10 times until you reach 20,480. By contrast our visual frequency range is between 400THz[3] (red light) up to 790THz for violet light which is slightly less than 1 octave.

Whilst it isn't necessary to be able to pull a wavelength out of your head for any given frequency it is helpful to remember these key values for room temperature air:

1kHz (1000Hz) has a wavelength of 34.3cm (0.343m)

So a frequency ten time higher with a wavelength ten times shorter:

10kHz (10,000Hz) has a wavelength of 3.43cm (0.0343m)

And a frequency ten times lower will have a wavelength ten times longer:

100Hz has a wavelength of 3.43m.

This helpful rule of thumb can help you to visualise size of the waves in the air and thus the behaviour of different frequencies in the air as you work.

The way sound interacts with the environment is heavily dependent on wavelength: short wavelengths are easily blocked or absorbed by small objects which have little or no effect on long wavelengths. So it is important to keep in mind the wavelengths of sound when considering their behaviour.

Sound waves are very obviously a three dimensional thing; they propagate away from their source in all directions until they encounter

---

2   For healthy young adult the audible frequency range is said to 20Hz to 20kHz although this varies between individuals and the upper range can degrade quite rapidly with age. Additionally left and right ears on the same person have different ranges.

3   Terahertz 1012 or 1 000 000 000 000 Hz. So Red light has a frequency of around 400 x1012 or 400 000 000 000 000Hz. Another fact you're unlikely to need but is quite interesting.

a change in the medium – often this is an obstacle such as a wall. Representing this three-dimensionality is difficult and very often such a level of complexity isn't required. A very common way of 'drawing' a sound wave is like this:

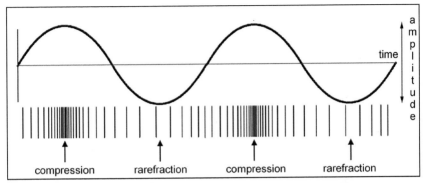

Fig 2.3 Amplitude/time graph of a sine wave.

Here a simple x-y graph is used with time represented horizontally (the x-axis) and amplitude (also called magnitude) represented vertically (the y-axis). Below it I have shown how this relates to the regions of high and low pressure in a simple pure-tone wave. This pure-tone, such as that generated by a tuning fork is called a sine-wave.

But while this graph has been drawn to represent the changes in air pressure, it could equally represent the electrical current in a loudspeaker cable or microphone cable that's carrying this same signal. It could even represent the movement of the loudspeaker cone or microphone diaphragm itself. As such it is a very helpful analysis tool.

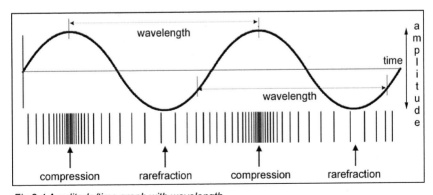

Fig 2.4 Amplitude/time graph with wavelength.

So we can also look at wavelength in this way, as the distance between any two identical points on successive waves as shown in fig. 2.4.

The amplitude (or magnitude) of a wave is basically how big it is and how we measure this depends on what we are doing with it at the time.

If we are looking at the 'wave' as a signal in a loudspeaker or microphone cable then we might measure it in volts or amps. We'll look at this in more detail in the next chapter on electricity.

If we are measuring the wave's amplitude in air then we measure it as variations in pressure, which we call Sound Pressure Level or SPL.

The standard unit of pressure is the Pascal (pa)[4] and the smallest pressure variation that we can hear is a minute 20μPa (twenty micropascals – see Table 4.3 in chapter 4). This variation causes a movement in your eardrum no bigger than the diameter of a single atom! By contrast the sound produced by a jet engine at close range is 20Pa which is a million times greater pressure variation.

Dealing with a range of numbers from 0.00002 to 20 is quite tedious, so a logarithmic system was devised which condenses this whole range into 0 to 120. We'll take a brief look at how logarithms work (for those that are interested) a little bit later on, but for now all we need to know is that this is called the decibel[5] scale.

Most texts give you a table such as this and some are quite comical in their choice of examples and all vary widely with the same examples. One book listed a cannery as having an SPL of 90dB. Personally I have no immediate recollection of being inside a cannery to make a meaningful comparison!

This is intended as a guide only as the examples shown vary widely depending on the circumstances – for example a smaller two engine jet plane makes much less noise than a four engine jumbo and 'normal conversation' varies widely as we automatically adjust to our environment, so a hushed conversation in a museum will be held at much lower levels than a meeting in a busy office.

It is worth investing in a reasonable budget SPL meter (see chapter on fault finding and test equipment) and familiarising yourself with various levels. However, don't forget that our ears, like our eyes vary their sensitivity and you can become accustomed to high ambient sound level so that it will be perceived as normal and you forget how loud it really is. The only way to accurately measure sound pressure is with an SPL meter in the same

---

4   A pascal is the SI unit of pressure equal to 1 newton of force per square metre. 1 newton is roughly 0.1 Kg.

5   The bel was named after Alexander Graham Bell and a deci bel is 1/10th of a bell. See Chapter 6.

way that only way to accurately measure how bright a room is, is to use a light meter.

Once sound waves leave the source device and before they reach the receiver (such as your ears or a microphone) there are five things that can happen to them and the effects all vary with frequency. They can be:

- Dissipated – loose energy as they spread out through the air
- Reflected – strike a hard surface and rebound thus changing direction
- Absorbed – strike a (usually) soft surface which takes away some or all of their energy
- Refracted – change direction as they pass through a change of medium
- Diffracted – bent as they pass over or around certain objects

Example			dB spl	Sound Pressure Pa
			140	200
		Jet engines at 100m	130	63
			120	20
	Symphony orchestra at fff		110	6.3
		Traffic noise by a busy road	100	2
			90	0.63
	Symphony orchestra at f		80	0.2
			70	0.063
Domestic TV listening level		Normal conversation (depending on environment	60	0.02
			50	0.0063
Empty theatre	Symphony orchestra at ppp		40	0.002
		Quiet rural house	30	0.00063
Quiet recording studio			20	0.0002
			10	0.000063
Threshold of hearing at 1kHz			0	0.00002

Table 2.3 Examples of Sound Pressure Levels.

Dissipation

In most cases sound is a three dimensional phenomenon; it spreads out away from the source horizontally (in two dimensions) and vertically (as the third dimension) as distance increases. Every form of radiated energy behaves this way whether it's the sound from a violin, the light from a light-bulb or the heat from the Sun. I'll take the light from a light bulb as an example. Consider lighting falling onto a surface 1m square (1m x 1m) that we've placed 1m away from the light. If we then double the distance between the surface and the light bulb to 2m, the same amount of energy now falls onto an area 2m x 2m (4 square m), so that 1m square surface only gets ¼ of the energy it did when it was 1m away.

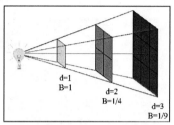

If we now move it to a distance of 3m the same energy now falls into an area 3m x 3m (9 square m), so that 1m square gets only $\frac{1}{9}$th of the original energy at 1m. If we carried on to a distance of 4m we'd find that same card receiving only $\frac{1}{16}$th of the energy. So every time we double the distance we reduce the energy falling onto a given area by a factor of four. This is called the inverse square law because

Fig. 2.5 Light-bulb example of the Inverse Square Law.

the energy received is proportional the inverse of the square of the distance:

$2^2 = 2 \times 2 = 4 \rightarrow ¼,$

$3^2 = 3 \times 3 = 9 \rightarrow \frac{1}{9}$

$4^2 = 4 \times 4 = 16 \rightarrow \frac{1}{16}$ etc.

For our purposes this translates to a 'loss' of 6dB every time we double the distance from a sound source, or a 'gain' of 6dB every time we half the distance to the source.

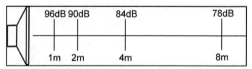

Taking this further we'd have 72dB at 16m, 66dB at 32m, 60dB at 64m and so on.

Fig 2.6 Example of Inverse Square Law in action over distance.

You can quickly calculate this with the following formula:

Level drop in dB = 20 x Log_{10} (change in distance)

Exceptions to this rule include sound contained in (for example) ventilation ducts where there is no increase in horizontal and vertical dimensions as the distance increases. Which is why these can be such a problem when they carry sound around a building. Cylindrical waves created by long sound sources such as noisy heating pipes or traffic on a busy motorway only spread out in two dimensions and so the reduction is only 3dB per doubling of distance. Line-source loudspeakers make use of this for wavelengths which are shorter than the longest dimension of the loudspeaker.

Reflection

When light hits a mirror it is reflected as shown in fig. 2.7

So it should come as no surprise that sound behaves in exactly the same way when it encounters a hard flat surface that is larger than its wavelength. When a precise reflection like this is produced, it can create 'ghost images', which produce

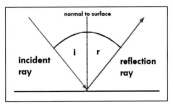

Fig 2.7 Light reflecting off a mirror.

the effect of a sound coming from within the reflective surface and, depending in the environment, can be almost as loud to a listener's ears then the actual sound they are trying to hear. As such this kind of 'hard reflection' can be very undesirable and consideration should be given in the design of listening rooms (be they concert halls, theatres or classrooms or whatever) to minimise these reflections – in practice is often isn't!

Hard concave surfaces can present a very difficult situation as they can serve to focus sounds into a certain area in a room. On the other hand, hard convex surfaces can be very effective diffusers. In fact before the invention of radar many concrete sound mirrors were built along England's east coast during the WW1, including Denge in Kent and Kilnsea in Yorkshire. These concave concrete structures focused the sound from enemy aircraft crossing the English Channel into a microphone. The Whispering Gallery in St Paul's Cathedral works in much the same way.

When sound strikes an uneven surface, the reflections fire off in all directions and are said to be diffusing. Such diffuse reflections can be very advantageous when used correctly as they preserve the energy of the sound which can be very useful in theatres and concert halls whilst not producing strong ghost images.

Absorption

When sound encounters a soft or porous surface some of it may be absorbed. I say 'may' because the extent to which this happens depends on the relationship between the surface and wavelength of the sound and also to what lies behind the soft or porous surface. In practice with many surfaces not specifically designed for acoustic treatments (and many that are) the actual result is a combination of reflection and absorption – and even some diffraction. There is a broad correlation between the thickness of an absorbing surface and the wavelengths it can effectively absorb. So if a hard concrete floor has soft carpet/underlay covering 25mm thick it will effectively absorb frequencies above about 3.4kHz falling away sharply at frequencies below that. This cut-off frequency coincides with the carpet/underlay being ¼ of the wavelength at about 3400Hz (3.4kHz). When you take up the carpet in room you will notice how much 'brighter' the room sounds – this is why.

In reality the situation is (as ever) much more complex than this simple analysis shows because carpet in not a uniform layer: it usually has a very soft 'pile' over a much harder backing which in turn sits on a soft underlay. The effect of this is usually to lower the effective absorption to maybe 1kHz or even lower. Sandwiching various densities of materials together can make very effective broadband absorbers but a detailed explanation of the performance and nature of various types of absorber is beyond the scope of this book. F. Alton Everest devotes over 50 pages to the topic in his book *Master Handbook of Acoustics*.

Diffraction and Refraction

Sound, like light, travels in straight lines, that is until it doesn't! Diffraction and Refraction are two effects which cause the direction in which the wave is travelling to change.

When light travels through a lens or a prism it is 'bent' – that is it changes direction. This happens because the light travels more slowly through the glass than it does through the air. In fact it's only about 0.0003 times slower – but that's enough to give us useful things like magnifying glasses, binoculars and spectacles. The same thing happens to sound waves as they change speed through different things and layers.

Just a few pages ago we looked at the different speed of sound through different air temperatures and the air around us is a complex mix of temperatures – even in relatively small rooms. Outdoors the air masses are larger but change temperature with altitude. A very common situation is shown here where, in the early morning the ground has started to warm up under the effect of sunlight but the air above it is still quite cool. This has the effect of refracting the sound up and away from the ground as the waves travel faster through the warmer air as shown in fig. 2.8.

In the evening the ground quickly radiates its heat after sunset and the air closer to ground cools more quickly than that higher up. In this case the sound is bent into the ground for the same reason as shown in fig. 2.9.

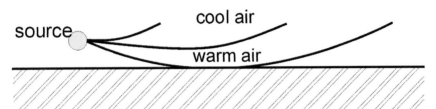

Fig 2.8 Sound refracted upwards by cool air layer over warm air layer.

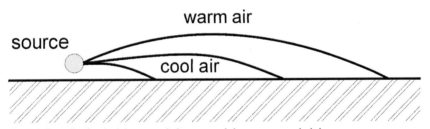

Fig 2.9 Sound refracted downwards by warm air layer over cool air layer.

Just to complicate this effect further, these masses can suddenly move – birds and glider pilots use thermals to gain height and a thermal is just a mass of warm air that takes off from the ground when it becomes too buoyant to stay down, just like a bubble in a pan of boiling water. Often these take off as a result of a stimulus, such as a moving vehicle. Cool air rapidly flows in underneath to fill the space and the result is that you have rapidly changing air temperature as well as rapid changes in air-flow and speed too. Such effects as this are transient and inconsistent, but don't be surprised by them when they do occur.

Sound will travel faster when its direction is superimposed into a stream of moving air. And, just to add another level of complication the flow of air is always slower closer to the ground thanks to friction between the fluid that is the air and the highly irregular surface that is the ground.

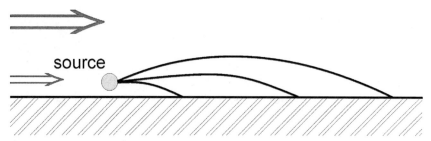

Fig 2.10 Sound refracted downwards by wind from behind the source.

So higher wind speeds above ground level cause the sound to bend into the ground when the wind comes from behind the source as shown in fig, 2.10

And it bends away from the ground when the wind blows towards the source as shown in fig. 2.11

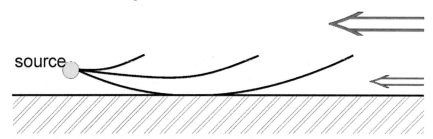

Fig 2.11 Sound refracted upwards by wind towards the source.

All these effects have the potential to cause massive changes to the way your sound reinforcement system behaves in the real world – and like so many situations, you have no control over it once it is in place. The best you can hope to do is to be aware of these problems at the design stage and attempt to manage the problems as best as possible within the constraints of the budget – but I guess that phrase applies to pretty much everything we do!

Interference

An important aspect of sound is what happens when two (or more) sound waves meet, especially if these sounds waves are basically identical but have taken different paths to get to a certain point. Examples of such a situation are when a direct sound and a reflected sound arrive at the ear of a listener. Or when two loudspeakers producing the same thing are heard together by a listener such as might happen if two loudspeakers are placed in close proximity. This diagram shows two sources producing two coherent waves.[6]

As you can see in fig 2.12 if the path lengths from sources A and B are identical then the two waves combine to give a result that is twice that of either component. But as the listener moves off to the side the path from source A gets progressively longer with respect to the path from source B. This has the effect that the resultant level diminishes and eventually each peak (+1 amplitude unit) from source A coincides with a trough (-1 amplitude unit) arriving at the same time from source B and the combination of the two waves results in zero.

The important point here is that this effect is frequency dependent; there will be complete cancellation (zero level) whenever the path lengths differ by an odd number of half wavelengths. So the effect will be repeated throughout the audio spectrum The result is often called comb filtering as the frequency response plot for any given point that is not equidistant from the two sources will resemble the teeth of a comb with deep troughs of attenuation where the two signals cancel each other out. How much of a problem this causes depends on the situation.

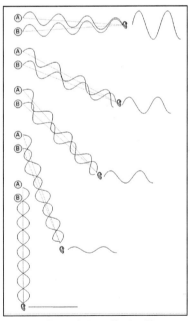

So the frequency response of the system for a position where the two paths are not identical will be something like that shown in fig 2.13. Hopefully you see where the name comb filtering comes from. Each trough corresponds to path length difference equivalent to an odd number of half wavelengths at that frequency and results in complete cancellation at that frequency.

However, frequency response graphs are more usually plotted with a logarithmic frequency scale where equal resolution (or detail) is given to each octave band or doubling of frequency. The same comb filter

Fig 2.12 Cancellation effects of two sources as a listener moves away from the centre line.

---

6 Coherent means identical form, in amplitude (level) and in step with each other – at least at the point of origin.

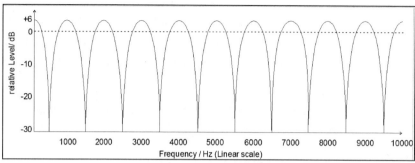

Fig. 2.13 'Comb filter' response plotted on a linear frequency graph.

response is shown on a logarithmic graph in fig 2.14. In this case the notion of the comb becomes rather hard to see.

It is important to realise that these effects not only affect the performance of two loudspeakers placed side by side, as mentioned above; it is also present when the sound from a loudspeaker is reflected off a wall or other surface but it is also present at the other end of the signal chain. So when the sound from a single source (such as an instrument) is picked up by two microphones then the same effect can be heard if those two microphones are mixed together into a single signal.

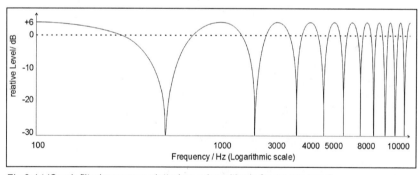

Fig 2.14 'Comb filter' response plotted on a logarithmic frequency graph.

How much of a problem these phenomena cause depends entirely on the situation in which they are observed. For example in a reasonably reverberant environment the comb filtering of multiple loudspeakers may well be almost completely lost once you move a comfortable distance away from them. In a situation with a close instrument mic and a more distant overhead mic (such as you might get with a drum kit) then the inverse-square law reduces the level to the distant mic and makes the comb-filter effect negligible. The important thing to realise is that when you do discover something odd in your well engineered sound system – you possess the understanding to figure out what is going on and hopefully you can find a solution. That solution may be as simple as moving a microphone slightly, or adjusting the position of a loudspeaker so as not to reflect off of a hard surface.

You can spend a lifetime studying the principles that I have only touched on in this chapter, and I would encourage you to do as much study as you can. However the basic principles described here should give enough of an insight into how sound behaves once it leaves the confines of an instrument or loudspeaker and starts on its journey to the listener's ears. I hope that you can appreciate that most of the 'damage' that is done to the signal chain is done in the acoustic environment rather in the electronic one.

3 MAKING IT LOUDER

There is evidence to suggest that ancient social groups numbered around 150 people[1], although estimates do vary quite widely. Since most of the human evolutionary ground work was done more than 250,000 years ago, it seems natural that we have evolved communications systems that can deal with groups of up to around this number. After all, most of us can easily address a group of about 150 people with a little practice – even if we're not comfortable doing it. Theatres of less than two hundred seats are regarded as intimate and do not usually require any amplification for speech reinforcement. However, as society developed and social groups increased in size, methods have evolved to increase the size of a group a voice can address – effectively by producing some sort of natural gain or increase in perceived level: the ancient theatres of the Romans and Greeks used reflective surfaces and carefully positioned the audience to direct 'early reflections' of the natural voice back into the audience and 'recycle' sound that would be lost in an totally open environment and so they could address many more people. This technique has been developed over years into theatres and halls that allow a suitably trained individual to comfortably address several thousand people. Instrument technology has also developed to produce devices that can project their sound more effectively with no greater effort on the part of the performer – if you ever get a chance, compare the sound from a modern concert grand piano to a period one from the time of Mozart or Beethoven.

Today we frequently have requirements for an individual or small group of people to successfully address many hundreds, thousands or even tens of thousands of people. Clearly this requires something more than just careful auditorium or instrument design.

Like so many modern 'things' that we often take from granted it is hard to pin down an exact timeline. The modern car for example started with horse-drawn carriages and adopted the internal combustion engine as chemical technology developed sufficiently to provide a liquid fuel. Then incremental engineering evolutions and developing manufacturing techniques eventually gave us something that we might recognise as a modern car which continues to evolve to suite new requirements. You

---

1   See the work of Robin Dunbar and Dunbar's number.

only have to look at a car from the early 20th Century to see its origins lie in horse-drawn coach-building.

PA systems have developed in a similar evolutionary fashion. This is by no means an exhaustive list, but here are a few highlights:

1870s First microphone invented

1877 Edison Phonograph invented

1904 First electronic valve is invented

1906 The 'audion' (first practical amplifier valve) is invented

1924 First moving coil, direct radiating loudspeaker patented

1933 First commercial compression driver introduced

1947 The transistor is invented

1959 First commercial integrated circuit launched

1957 Process for digital recording on a computer developed

1964 First electret microphone invented

1970 Digital to optical recording system patented – this lays the foundations for the compact disc.

Now we have come to expect high quality PA system capable of projecting high sound pressure levels across the entire human-audio bandwidth to audiences as large as it is possible to manage. In much the same way as I would like to see the reaction of the Nikolaus Otto or Karl Benz if they were to see a modern high speed super car, I would like to see the reactions of some of those early pioneers of reproduced sound, if they were to see and hear the capabilities of a modern concert sound system.

We have become more accustomed to the 'sound' of amplification and as an audience, often we expect it. That said, you only have to listen to the differences of opinion between (for example) musical theatre audiences who expect microphones and amplification and opera audiences to whom the concept of vocal amplification is often as abhorrent as custard on fish-and-chips to realise that differences of opinion vary widely; understanding the expectations of your audience is a great part of successful sound system design.

So a typical PA system has to perform one of two basic functions – or frequently both at the same time:

- To reproduce a previously recorded sound, or group of sounds (maybe a multi-channel backing track or recorded announcement).

- To reinforce a live sound as it is generated by a usually a voice (or voices) and/or instrument (or instruments).

In the latter case, the live sound has to be captured by some kind of transducer such as a microphone, unless it is already in 'an electronic format', such as an electronic keyboard. In the first case the sound-to-be is read from media, such as a computer hard-drive, optical disc (such as a CD) or some other storage media. The sound system takes this source and passes it through successive stages of amplification and processing before turning it back into acoustic energy through a loudspeaker system and before it passes into the listeners' ears.

Sometimes we want the sound to be up-front and powerful as part of the experience and sometimes we want to create the illusion of a totally natural sound that has no amplification whilst giving the performers all the help possible. Each has its challenges and must be considered during the design stage.

In the case of the transducers, their physical placement often has a massive impact on the quality of the reproduced sound and the success of the results. For example, microphone placement can change the tonal quality of the instrument. The pick-up switch on an electric guitar has a similar effect and all it does is select which of several (or which combination of) pick-ups is used, the ones closer to the bridge producing a sound which might be described as 'harder' than those closer to the fret board.

Physical placement of the loudspeakers makes the difference between a poor sound system design and successful one. As we read in the previous chapter, the vast majority of the signal degradation and corruption is done in the path between the loudspeaker and the listener.

So let's start at the beginning and consider the process of amplifying sound. A very simple case is often this:

microphone → pre-amplifier → mixer-amplifier → line-amplifier → power-amplifier → loudspeaker

The microphone (frequently abbreviated to mic) takes acoustic signals and turns them into electrical ones. There are many different types with many characteristics which make them more or less appropriate to a specific task.

The pre-amplifier raises the weak signals from the microphone to a more robust signal that can be handled by most other devices. Often this will have a gain control and/or range switch to allow use different types of microphone and different sources. It might also include a 'phantom power' switch for microphones that require a power supply – we'll look at all these aspects a bit later.

The mixer-amplifier stage combines as many different signals as you need. It is this stage which forms the core of the 'mixing console' that most people think off when they talk about sound engineering. This section is usually presented to the user as an array of 'faders' (which can be rotary controls or more frequently linear sliders). As such it can attenuate (reduce) your signals when the fader is below zero or amplify (increase) when above zero. In this way the fine balance (or mix) of individual instruments or other source can be controlled before being passed onto the next stage.

The line amplifier sends the final signal to the power amplifier. Often many line amplifiers are used to send signal to different sets of loudspeakers as well as recording devices, etc. Up to this point we are dealing with low voltages and minute currents.

The power amplifier then drives the loudspeakers – and now we start to get into higher electrical powers and the 'health and safety' considerations become increasingly important. The power amplifier has one of the hardest jobs in the electronic signal chain: loudspeakers are very complex electrical loads and yet are remarkably fragile when mistreated. To generate a loud kick-drum or other similar percussive sound requires a vast amount of transient energy spanning a surprising range of frequencies and a good power amplifier must be able to deliver that energy and yet return to a low quiescent, almost standby state immediately afterwards. We will see later on that the ratio of powers required to span the range of human hearing is in excess of a million-fold $(1,000,000$ or $10^6)$ and such changes need to be virtually instantaneous.

Frequently other devices are 'inserted' into this signal chain, such as equalisers (often just called EQ); these apply different amounts of gain to different frequency bands and so allow the 'tone' or 'colour' of the sound to be changed. Dynamic processors such as compressors apply varying amounts of gain to limit the level certain instruments can attain. Misuse of such systems is a fast way to destroy an otherwise good mix! But all these will be examined later on.

So we see can how the signal increases as it passes through the various stages:

mic		pre-amp		mix-stage		line-amp		power-amp
~2mV	→	~1V	→	~1V	→	~1V	→	20V to 100V and more[2]

So systems for reproducing sound – either for reinforcing a 'live' sound or replaying a previously 'stored' sound - can vary in size and complexity from a simple one-box mixer-amplifier built into the back of a small loudspeaker up to systems needing several large trucks to transport them. However the basic principles that dictate their use and operations are identical and one of the initial design criteria when specifying any kind of audio reproduction system is how big does it need to be. In chapter 7 we will look at a simple step-by-step approach to the specification of a loudspeaker system.

In the next few chapters we will look at some of the basic engineering principles necessary for live sound engineering: electricity, acoustics and how they are referenced (decibels) before we start to look at the more specific principles of how loudspeakers work and how to use them – as well as microphones and mixers.

4 ELECTRONIC BASICS

Electricity is a form of energy and as such it can do work: it can boil a kettle, light an otherwise dark room, it can melt steel or open a door. It is the most useful type of energy we know of: small amounts of it can be coded to carry information around the planet or just across the room yet it powers and controls the vast machines of industry. It is also important to remember that, when not treated with the utmost care, it can be lethal.

All sound recording, reproduction and reinforcement systems use the coding ability of electricity: sound waves entering a microphone are converted into electrical signals which pass through a number of devices (which usually make the signals bigger and less susceptible to noise and interference) before being converted back into larger sound waves with an amplifier and loudspeaker. They may well be stored somewhere along the way – such as being recorded for reproduction hours, days, or even years later, or just to make them wait a short while to allow other things to catch up. For example, video signals on a display screen of some sort usually take longer to process (and the more switching and processing that is done the longer the process takes) and so the audio signals need to be delayed by a short while otherwise you notice that people's lips on the screen don't match up with the words you're hearing.

Devices which convert sound (or any mechanical energy) to electricity and vice versa are called transducers. We (as sound engineers) use the term microphone (mic or mike for short) for devices which take in sound and make electricity and loudspeaker (or 'speaker) for those which take in electricity and make sound; headphones and earphones are essentially very small loudspeakers but they work in exactly the same way.

The study of electronics is a vast and complex field which many people find engaging and rewarding, but for our purposes of sound engineering we only require a basic level of knowledge to begin with – and indeed many people go on to have very long and rewarding careers in the sound industry with little or no knowledge of electronics at all. I believe that the more you know about the 'nuts and bolts' of your world the better you can interact with it – the more you understand how a car works the better you can handle it – especially when it does something unexpected, so a bit of basic electronics along with some basic acoustics will help you as a sound engineer in the same way.

What is Electricity

Electricity can be visualised as a flow of energy and is often (and with good reason) compared to the flow of water. With water flowing in a pipe, molecules of water (H_2O) push each other along the pipe in the direction of the flow. Putting water into one end of a full pipe causes a virtually instant appearance of water at the other end – even though it won't be the same water. In the case of electricity, the particles, called electrons[1] move between atoms in the wire-conductor. Each electron carries a minute but finite amount of energy – if you want to move a lot of them (with a high current) you need a big pipe – a thick piece of wire.

As with any flow there is energy carried which is proportional to the pressure and rate of flow of this fluid. So we can deliver enough energy to melt steel on the one hand or transmit massive amounts of data across the globe with tiny amounts of electricity using a device that can run for hours or even days on a small battery.

Electricity flows from points of higher potential to points of lower potential like water naturally flows from higher levels to lower levels. This is why birds can sit on high voltage power lines without being electrocuted – the cable and the bird are at the same potential so there is no path for the electricity to flow along. If a bird were to make contact with both the wire and the earthed metal pylon or bridge the gap between two wires, then there would be a very large potential difference and a large current would make for a toasted bird!

Electrical Term	Water Analogy	Unit	Symbol	Description
potential difference	pressure	volt	V	The force behind the flow.
charge	quantity	coulomb	C	the amount of flow
current	rate of flow	amp	A	Flow rate (per unit of time) – 1 amp is 1 coulomb per second

---

1   Electrons are named after the Greek word for amber which the ancient Greeks used to generate static electricity. The electrons actually flow from the negative (or point of lower potential) to positive (or point of higher potential). We conventionally think of electricity flowing from positive (or point of higher potential) to negative (or point or lower potential). The reason for this is that electrons are actually negatively charged particles which can move from atom to atom in a conducting material. By the time it was realised that this was how it all happened, the naming conventions had been established and so we're stuck with it.

Electrical Term	Water Analogy	Unit	Symbol	Description
resistance	friction	ohm	Ω	resistance to flow – similar to friction
energy	energy	joule	J	The energy carried by anything, water and electricity being just two examples
power	power	watt	W	Rate of energy conversion (per unit of time) - 1 watt is 1 joule per second

Table 4.1 Comparison between electrical flow and water flow.

Table 4.1 compares the parameters of electrical flow and water flow. For the most part we only need concern ourselves with:

- voltage (more correctly called potential difference) – unit of electrical pressure (volts)
- current – unit of electrical 'quantity' (amps)
- Resistance/Impedance – effectively electrical 'friction' how difficult is the flow of electricity - Unit Ohms.
- Power – how much electrical energy we are 'using' at any given time – unit Watts.

Electrical Relationships?

There are a few equations (sorry) that is it worth trying to remember. The first being Ohm's law which states this:

$$V = IR \text{ (or often } V = IZ)$$

The R strictly refers to resistance (in DC circuits) and the latter 'Z' referring to impedance in the more complex case of AC circuits. For now I will refer to Resistance accepting that this is technically incorrect in the majority of cases but for now it illustrates the point.

This can be rearranged to:

$$I = V/R \text{ or } R = V/I$$

Putting that into words:

$V = IR \rightarrow$ Voltage (volts) equals current (amps) multiplied by Resistance (ohms)

$R = V/I \rightarrow$ Resistance (ohms) equals voltage (volts) divided by current (amps)

$I = V/R \rightarrow$ Current (amps) equals voltage (volts) divided by resistance (ohms)

So you can calculate voltage if you know current and resistance (or impedance) or current if you know voltage and impedance, etc.

We also have the formula $P = VI$, which defines electrical power as the product of voltage and current. And this can be rearranged to:

$V = P/I$ and $I = P/V$.

Putting this into words:

$P = VI \rightarrow$ Power (watts) is equal to voltage (volts) multiplied by current (amps)

$V = P/V \rightarrow$ Voltage (volts) is equal to power (watts) divided by current (amps)

$I = V/R \rightarrow$ Current (amps) is equal to power (watts) divided by voltage (volts)

If you want to go further you can combine these equations into this lot, but a thorough discussion of all this is beyond the scope of this book.

$V = IR$	$V = P/I$	$V = \sqrt{(PR)}$
$I = V/R$	$I = \sqrt{(P/R)}$	$I = P/V$
$R = V^2/P$	$R = P/I^2$	$R = V/I$
$P = V^2/R$	$P = I^2R$	$P = VI$

Table 4.2 – Common electrical relationship equations.

Resistance or Impedance

Strictly speaking resistance concerns DC currents (ones that are constant and do not change or at least change very slowly) whereas impedance concerns AC currents (like audio signals) where the changes of voltages and currents happen quickly and as a result do not always follow each other exactly. For example, the impedance of a low pass filter in a loudspeaker crossover is designed to rise above that point which prevents high frequencies from entering the low frequency driver of the loudspeaker.

Detailed AC theory is a complex topic that we only dip into in this text, for our purposes it is sufficient to understand these basics but also to be aware that some things are not necessarily as simple as they might appear. For example, if you put a multimeter[2] across an 8Ω loudspeaker driver you are measuring the DC resistance which is likely to be about 6Ω or less. This doesn't mean that the impedance is wrong – 8Ω is usually qualified as nominal impedance which is a kind of best-fit average. As the cone or diaphragm moves under the influence of the electrical current applied to it, then its motion will also be affected by the suspension (the various methods used to hold it in place which behave like springs), its weight, and the mass of the air it is moving both inside and outside the box it is enclosed in (assuming it is in an enclosure of some sort). It might actually have an impedance of 8 Ohms at only a few specific frequencies, over the rest of its operating range it might drop as low as three or four ohms, and rise to ten ohms or more. Once it rises above this then it is pretty much outside its usable frequency range as it ceases to become efficient.

Units and Multipliers

At this point, it worth mentioning the use of standard engineering multiples which is a system of common multipliers that has been developed to cope with the vast range of things that we meet in all types of engineering. These are prefixed to practically any unit you care to think about such as kilometres being 1000 metres. See table 4.3.

Practical applications

For our purposes a general knowledge of these principles is sufficient to offer a clearer view of our working lives as sound engineers. For example:

If we have a 1000W amplifier and speaker combination, with an 8 ohm loudspeaker, then we can calculate that the current in the loudspeaker cable will be over 11 amps! So it is very important to have good quality high-current loudspeaker cable.

If you have a 16A 240V mains supply to your mixing console position in a venue than we have a limit of 3,840 watts, which is a good reason not to connect a kettle (typically 2kW to 3kW) as that doesn't leave very much for all your gear.

A dynamic microphone which generates 50mV into 600ohms is a current of only about 80 microamps. Hence we need to treat these

---

2 A multimeter is another essential item of test equipment that should be in every toolbox. It allows basic measurements of (at least) voltage, current, resistance and continuity. See chapter 15 on fault finding and essential test equipment

signals with great care as they can be easily wiped out with induced electrical noise from adjacent power cables and switch gear.

The faster a voltage is changed the higher the current flow will be. So to generate the really fast pulses needed for digital audio and similar data applications the greater the current and so the greater the load on the power supply – this is why digital signal processing tends to run hotter than it's analogue equivalent and why faster computers generate more heat and need bigger power supplies than their slower comrades.

Name	Symbol	Factor	Shorthand	Example
pico	p	÷ 1,000,000,000,000	10^{-12}	
nano	n	÷ 1,000,000,000	10^{-9}	One Billionth of a metre. Around the wavelength of visible light
micro	μ	÷ 1,000,000	10^{-6}	Microvolt: one millionth of a volt
milli	m	÷ 1,000	10^{-3}	Millimetre: one thousandth of a metre
kilo	k	× 1,000	$. 10^{3}$	Kilometre: one thousand metres
mega	M	× 1,000,000	10^{6}	Megawatt: one million watts
giga	G	× 1,000,000,000	10^{9}	Gigabits: one billion bits of data. Often used to describe network data speeds
tera	T	× 1,000,000,000,000	10^{12}	Four Hundred Terahertz is around the frequency of red light

Table 4.3.

Balanced and Unbalanced Signals

You will notice that most of the connectors used for low level signals be they from microphones to mixers or from mixers or other processing devices to amplifiers have three connection (or terminals) in them such as the XLR connectors in fig.4.1. Whilst others that might connect more domestic equipment like CD players have only two like the RCA/phono connectors shown in fig. 4.2. The ubiquitous ¼" jack plug can be balanced (3 pole) or unbalanced (2 pole) as shown in fig. 4.3. The 2 pole types are often called mono jacks and the 3 pole types are often called stereo. In professional audio (with the exception of headphones) the 3 pole jacks are very rarely used for stereo signals.

The basic difference between balanced and unbalanced signal lines is how the return current path is handled. In an unbalanced system the return current passes back through screen (or shield). In a balanced system the return current passes through separate line with the send and return as a twisted-pair cable. This makes balanced lines much less susceptible to induced noise. For example, most telephone systems don't use screened cable for their signal distribution and yet they are extremely quiet, considering the length of cabling and the environment they work in. This is because they use balanced lines. Most Ethernet networks use UTP cable which is four pairs of balanced twisted pair cable with no screen. Usually the signal which is the same polarity as the original signal is called the hot and the inverted signal is called the cold. By convention on an XLR connector pin 1 carries the ground or shield, pin 2 is the hot and pin 3 is the cold. Perhaps counter intuitively, the signal output connector is the male.

Fig. 4.1 Three-pin XLR connectors for balanced signals.

Fig. 4.2 RCA Phono connector – a single pin with a wrap-around screen.

Fig. 4.3 ¼" jack plugs: 2 Pole (mono) top and 3 pole (stereo) above.

With a balanced signal in a twisted pair cable any external noise is induced identically onto both 'legs' of the twisted pair i.e. the same noise gets onto both conductors in the pair at the same level and same phase. When this signal arrives at what's called a differential input, the differential input stage only looks at the difference between the two legs and noise is effectively cancelled out, see fig. 4.4. The 'hot' is shown in red and the 'cold' in blue. When the balanced (differential) input stage inverts the cold and adds it to the hot, the noise which is symmetrical on both lines gets inverted on the cold and is then cancelled out. The degree of rejection by a differential input stage is called common mode rejection ratio or CMRR and

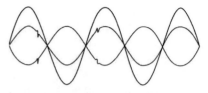

Fig. 4.4 Noise spikes cancelled out by balance line and input stage.

is expressed as a ratio in dB which is the effective rejection of such noise.

Typically balanced lines drive into lower impedances than unbalanced lines which make them even less susceptible to noise. This is due to the signal current being higher and thus induced noise, which is typically high voltage-very low current, has less effect. Transformers are entirely current dependant devices and so form the basis of high quality input stages. Transformers can also serve to isolate the signal lines from the signal ground and offer yet more ways to reduce noise.

Earthing or Grounding Considerations

Theoretically, with good common-mode rejection a fully balanced system needs no screen or shield - after all most telecommunications systems function without one for considerable sections of their cabling systems and most computer networks use UTP (unshielded twisted pair) cabling. The secret is that the balanced links do not directly reference to ground and so any induced noise is ignored by the balanced input stage.

As we have just discussed, in unbalanced systems the ground becomes the return path for the signal current. This system works fine in the protected environment inside the casing of your electronic thingy (mostly) but far less so in the hostile RF and hum-field saturated world outside. By using screened or shielded cable you are effectively extending the metal casing around the signal path and going some way to protecting your signal integrity. However as cable lengths increase and external noise rises so does the ability of this noise to get into your signal cable and also into the shield itself. Either of these situations adds noise to your signal. The solution is to only use balanced systems and if you have unbalanced inputs or outputs – balance them! This can be achieved either with electronic line drivers or simple line-balancing transformers.

The screen achieves two things:

- It protects the signal from picking up noise from outside.

- It stops your signal from radiating out of the cable and becoming noise to somebody else.

In fact good twisted pair cable and line balancing achieves both of these too, so the screen is just there to help. On the second point, the frequencies encountered in audio signals are so low (compared to RF signals) that their wavelength makes even the longest practical audio cable very inefficient transmission aerials, however noise induced by much higher frequency processor clocks, etc. in digital audio equipment can cause radiation problems on much shorter cable runs. So screens are provided which should be nothing more than the continuation of the metal casing around the equipment. i.e. the screen should be wired to the casing and stay as far away from the signal path as possible. That said there are occasionally problems caused by mixing balanced and unbalanced systems and even some pieces of equipment that do not take their screening and signal-earthing as seriously as they should and you wind up with a system buzz. We will look at how to deal with this in chapter 15 on fault finding.

Loudspeaker Connections

As we discussed earlier, loudspeakers take quite high voltages and currents and the connectors used need to reflect this. Most of the loudspeaker connectors that you'll meet in professional audio loudspeakers are the Neutrik Speakon in NL4 (4 pin) version Fig. 4.5, and NL8 (8 pin version) Fig. 4.6 and the Cannon EP (metal chassis) Fig 4.7 or AP (plastic chassis) Fig. 4.8. The AP/EP could be anything from 4 pin all the way up to 8 pin depending on the loudspeaker system and the configuration.

Fig. 4.5 NL4 'Speakon'.

Generally NL4 and EP/AP4 and EP/AP5 are used for passive systems where only two conductors are required and for 2-way active systems where four conductors are required. NL8s and EP/AP6 and EP/AP8s are used for multiway systems where up to eight conductors are needed. See chapter 11 for a discussion on active loudspeaker systems.

Fig. 4.6 NL8 'Speakon'.

Fig. 4.7 EP5 connector.

Fig. 4.8 AP4 connector.

Both these types of connector are pretty robust and can handle the large currents required for high powered loudsopeakers.

5 ACOUSTICS AND THE SPACE

In these days of computer design and automatic production techniques it is possible to design and build loudspeakers and electronics system to a very high level of quality and sophistication. I have said this before but I will repeat myself, by far the most of the damage done to the audio signal path is in the physical domain between the loudspeaker and the ear or the source and the microphone as the sound passes through the air. Whilst an in-depth explanation of room acoustics is beyond the scope of this book and a student can spend his entire life studying this fascinating field we will attempt to provide a basic understanding that will aid the sound engineer in his daily work and provide the basis for further study if needed.

As we've seen in chapter 2, sound from a source dissipates through three dimensional space and the energy decreases with the square of the distance, which is called the inverse square law. So the level drop can be calculated as $dB = 20 \times Log_{10}$ (change in distance). In an open space (such as outdoors) this process continues until the energy is so low as to be inaudible as it falls below the background noise or ambient level.

In special rooms (called anechoic chambers) the same thing happens as all the energy that falls onto the walls and other surfaces is completely absorbed. In all other environments – which will form most of our working lives as sound engineers – some of the energy will be reflected and some will be absorbed. If a large amount of energy is absorbed and very little is reflected then we say the room is a 'dead room' and if a lot of energy is reflected which then goes on to be re-reflected and so on then we say the room is 'live' or 'reverberant'.

Eventually all of the acoustic sound energy in a given environment will be lost as minute amounts of heat; as sound travels through any media be it air, steel or fabric, it warms that media up very, very slightly and loses energy in the process.[1]

Excessive reverberation caused by high levels of reflected acoustic

---

1 Thus contributing the gradual increase in entropy that defines the 'arrow of time', or human perception of cause and effect and the fate of our universe. See work by Arthur Eddington, Albert Einstein, Stephen Hawking and many, many more. Please note that none of this has very much to do with sound engineering!

energy is detrimental to the quality of the sound we are trying to work with. Conversely very 'dead' environments with virtually no reflected energy are also very difficult to work with but in differing ways.

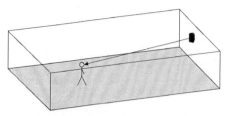

Fig. 5.1 Only direct sound reaches the listener.

Fig. 5.1 shows very dead room with only the direct sound from a loudspeaker being heard by the listener. And the phrase "The cat sat on the mat" would look like fig 5.2 on a recording trace at the listener's ear when heard in this room.

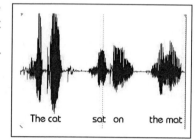

Fig. 5.2 Anechoic amplitude/time trace of a simple phrase.

Compare this with a very reflective room like the one in fig 5.3 where the sound from the loudspeaker is reflected many times. The listener will hear the same sound every time it passes his or her ear over a prolonged period of time compared to the direct-only sound example above.

In this case the same phrase will appear like fig 5.4 recording trace at the listener's ear.

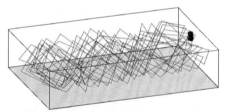

Fig. 5.3 The listener hears a lot of strong reflections after the direct sound

As you can see in fig 5.4 it is impossible to see the individual words in this trace compared to the last one and it should come as no surprise that it is very difficult to hear the individual words; the start of each new word is masked by the decaying sound of the previous one(s). The same is true of music in this environment. For some types of music, this is beneficial and such music has been written

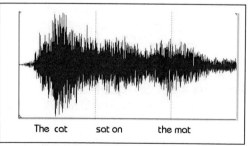

Fig. 5.4 Reverberant amplitude/time trace of the same simple phrase.

to be heard in this kind of environment. Examples are some choral or organ music. But any rapid passages are lost to the listener. Have a look at the effect of the same two environments on four fairly rapid kick-drum beats:

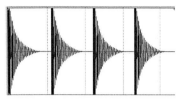

On the trace in fig 5.5 you can see the natural and rapid decay of the four

Fig. 5.5 Anechoic amplitude/time trace of four kick-drum beats.

distinct sounds of four hits on a kick drum. On the trace in fig 5.6 the distinct 'beats' are lost so any real sense of rhythm would be lost too.

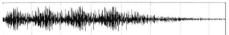

Fig. 5.6 Reverberant amplitude/time trace of four kick-drum beats.

Reverberation time is the term used to quantify the amount of reverberation in a room. The standard measurement we have now dates back to the work done by W.C. Sabine in the 19th century and is based on the time it takes for a given sound to decay to a level of inaudibility. Sabine found that this reduction was typically about 60dB. Consequently we now have RT_{60} as a standard measure of reverberation time. So the RT_{60} of a room is the time takes a sound to decay by 60dB. In the real world making such measurements over a 60dB range can be difficult and so measurements are frequently taken using a decay of say 30dB or 40dB and the decay graph is extrapolated to meet the 60dB line and the value read off. Many professionals now advocate the use of RT_{30} measurements (which can then be extrapolated to RT_{60}) as this avoids some complexities in room response at low listening levels towards the end of the RT_{60} tail.

Simple broadband time values can give an idea as to the room, but since lower frequencies (with longer wavelengths) are more difficult to absorb, they usually have longer reverberation times than higher frequency (shorter wavelength) sounds in the same space.

Fig 5.7 shows a rather stepped 'curve' is the

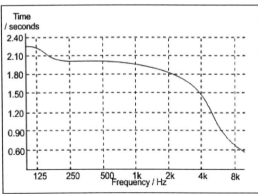

Fig 5.7 Real concert hall reverberation variation with frequency.

reverberation time for specific frequencies of a well-known concert hall in England. It clearly shows a reverberation time of over two seconds for frequencies below 250Hz and yet a time of below one second for frequencies above 6kHz. Each room will have its own characteristic reverberation time signature curve and is one principle reason that makes them all sound different.

So we define a reverberant environment as one in which multiple paths all of different lengths arrive at the listeners' ears over a period of time; the longer the time that these reflections remain audible (which is due to a high energy transfer in each reflection) the more reverberant the space. A 'nice' reverberation is one in which all of the reflections are smeared evenly over a reasonable period of time and die away in a reasonably even way (with respect to frequency). A not so 'nice' reverberation is one where there are particularly defined reflections (say from a hard curved wall) or with peaks at certain frequencies that stand out almost as loud as the original sound. I am reminded of a particular theatre which has a hard concrete wall at the rear of the seating area which curved in such a way as to reflect individual instruments in the orchestra. If you walk from the stage to the back of the auditorium you will perceive various instruments in turn reflected louder from the back wall than the natural sound from the orchestra pit behind you.

One important feature of reverberant field which might not be obvious is that, because it is composed of many, many reflections from all around the room (the more the better) it exists at an even level throughout the room, falling away at a constant rate throughout the space, whereas the direct sound obeys the inverse square law and falls by 6dB for each doubling of distance.

Direct to reverberant field

So you might think that pure direct sound (that is sound free of any secondary reflections or reverberation) is the ideal target for an audience and that anything else is coloured or less than ideal, but actually the real world situation is rather more complex than this. It turns out that our ear brain system is not only remarkably good at filtering out the direct sound from the complex mix of reflection and reverberation but that it actually needs a lot of additional 'stuff' to help it out. Obviously in a musical environment a 'nice' reverberation can make a good performance outstanding; the sound of last note(s) persisting slightly into the next one(s) brings the performance alive. If you listen to a purely acoustic orchestra on an outdoor stage where there is no natural reverberation, even the best performance can sound a little dull and lifeless. Worse still the conductor and the musicians will find the performance very difficult and are often uninspired for the very same reason and will subconsciously give a lesser performance then they might in a well designed concert hall with a lively acoustic. This isn't to question their professionalism, it is just that we all perform better when we're in a pleasing environment. There are a number of recordings of orchestras playing in anechoic chambers and they are well worth spending a little time listening to so as to appreciate just how weird they sound.

On the other hand deciding exactly how much is a 'good amount' of reverberation depends on what is going on. For example some RT_{60}s are:

- Symphonic Concert Halls are around 2 to 2.5 seconds.
- Theatres are around 1 to 1.5 seconds if they include both musical and speech performances.
- Lecture theatres are typically 0.9 seconds and are designed for high intelligibility speech only.
- Traditional churches and cathedrals can be as high 10 seconds or more. This may seem odd but don't forget that for many years Christian worship was not based on the spoken word but on sung worship. In addition, The Reformation saw the removal of decorative wooden panelling and so forth which would have made this situation worse.

If you try to speak to even a modest group of people on an RT_{60} of significantly less than 0.9, the room sounds dry and you (the presenter) feel isolated. In addition this short RT_{60} (of 0.9s) actually helps the intelligibility.

Haas and Precedence

In fact we have evolved an incredibly efficient internal filter that is able to extract the direct sound from the reflected sound arrivals. As long ago as the 1951 Helmut Haas was investigating the effect of reflections (or echoes) on speech for his PhD thesis. This research has been carried forward by many researches using ever more sophisticated technology and reaching ever more detailed conclusions.

Haas found that a delayed secondary sound (reproduced by a second loudspeaker) delayed by between 5ms and 30ms had to be around 10dB louder if before it was perceived as a secondary 'echo'. Similar research by Olive & Toole (1989), Lochner & Burger (1958) and Meyer & Schodder (1952) has found broadly similar results which I have attempted to superimpose into one diagram in fig 5.8. Some of these tests were testing subtly different things but for our purposes secondary 'reflections' in the lower shaded region can be ignored as you (or your audience) are very unlikely to notice them. In the unshaded region listeners will experience a change in acoustic perception described by test subjects as spaciousness or broadening which is a blurring of the direction of the source – as is often the case in a room with some reverberation over a purely dead room.

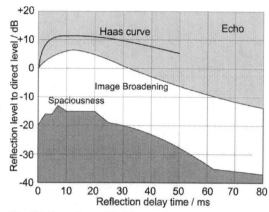

Fig. 5.8 Haas Curve (1951) superimposed onto other research by Meyer & Schodder (1952), Lochner & Burgur (1958), Olive & Toole (1989).

In the upper shaded region the listener is very likely to hear reflections or secondary arrivals as real echoes. We will look at this research later on when we look at time alignment of loudspeaker systems.

The basic premise of all of this research is that a secondary arrival (such as a reflection) that arrives within 5 to 30 ms of the original direct sound can be up to 10 dB louder than the direct sound without being perceived as an actual echo. So 'nice' acoustic environments aim to have all the 'early reflections' arrive at the listener within this 30ms window of the direct sound. To put it another way, if the direct sound arrives at the listener after 150ms (just over 50m) then all of the direct reflections should ideally arrive within 180ms. After this time the reflections should have become so numerous that they can no longer be heard as individual sounds and have become reverberation – which can persist for several seconds. If you get the chance, try 'playing' with a good electronic reverberation unit and see what the effect is on both simple music (where you can hear details) and a single voice from a microphone. By good I mean one where you have access to the parameters of early reflections and decay time. The better ones give you several curve ranges (as in the concert hall graph example above) where you can define separate times for each frequency range to best achieve the effect you desire. In fact as a general rule always try to find time to familiarise yourself with such equipment before letting yourself and it loose in a live environment.

We can still extract useful information out of the reverberant field even when the direct sound has actually fallen to a level of less than that of the

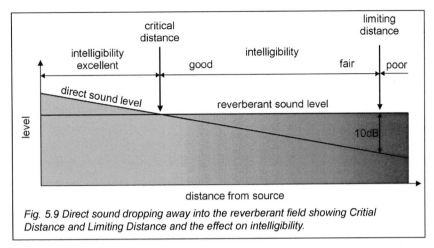

Fig. 5.9 Direct sound dropping away into the reverberant field showing Critial Distance and Limiting Distance and the effect on intelligibility.

reverberant sound. This simplified diagram fig. 5.9 shows how the direct sound level and reverberant field level varies as you move away from the direct sound source.

Let's imagine that a loudspeaker is reproducing the sound of somebody reading some text from a book (for example).[2] The listener is walking in a straight line away from the loudspeaker in a reasonably reverberant environment. This simplified diagram fig 5.9 shows how a listener will perceive the voice that he/she hears from the loudspeaker:

As long as the dominant sound is that of the direct sound, then the intelligibility will be excellent and the listener should have no problems in hearing every word.

As the distance increases then direct sound falls (by the inverse square law), but the reverberant field doesn't – it is constant throughout the room. When the direct sound and the reverberant sound are at the same level we have reached critical distance. Intelligibility is still good at this point.

As the listener moves still further away the direct sound continues to fall (by the inverse square law) but the reverberant field stays constant, and the intelligibility starts to decline. Eventually when the distance away from the loudspeaker is three times the critical distance then we reach a point where the direct sound is 10dB below the reverberant field and

---

2   Speech intelligibility is relatively easy to measure (in comparison to many of the other subjective assessments used for comparing audio system quality!) However it remains an excellent test as to the overall performance of a sound reinforcement system. Traditionally it is done by asking a representative sample of people to write down words that are spoken to them and then looking at the percentage of correct words.

the useful intelligibility has effectively dropped to zero. This is called the limiting distance.

So in a real world test you can find the critical distance with nothing more technical than a simple budget hand-held sound pressure meter (SPL meter). To do this set up a a loudspeaker and play either a low dynamic music track (i.e. one which doesn't vary much in level) or perhaps better some pink noise at a reasonable level – say 20dB above ambient (measured at some convenient distance from the loudspeaker but no closer than 1m away) then walk slowly away from the loudspeaker. As you do this you will notice the SPL drop by 6dB at twice the distance and again at four times the distance by the inverse square law. There should come a point where the level stops dropping (unless you are out doors or in some other anechoic environment). As you can see from the diagram when the direct sound and the reverberant sound are at the same level then you have found critical distance. Your limiting distance is then simply this distance times by three. So, if your SPL meter 'levels out' at 10m (critical distance) then your limiting distance is 30m.

It is worth mentioning that it can be relatively easy to add electronic reverberation to a dry environment but it impossible to remove reverberation electronically from an overly live environment. The only way to 'tame' an over reverberant environment is to actually absorb the excess energy using curtains, acoustic foam, tuned absorbers and other means. On the other hand, whilst you can't change the acoustic environment, you can avoid making a difficult situation worse by careful selection of loudspeaker; using a more directive loudspeaker (often called a high 'Q' loudspeaker) to focus the energy at your listeners will avoid exciting the reverberation field in the room and thus improve the direct to diffuse ratio.

By doing this we can move the critical distance further away from the loudspeaker and give a better listening experience to more listeners as shown in fig. 5.10.

We look at how to make the choice of loudspeakers in chapter 7.

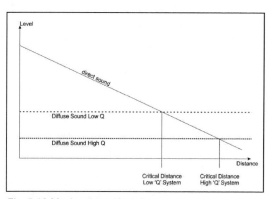

Fig. 5.10 Moving the critical distance by using more directional loudspeakers.

6 DECIBELS

At this point I am going to take a few minutes to discuss decibels. We have used them a few times in preceding chapters and we will use them more and more in later chapters. I think that decibels are probably one of the most misunderstood terms in sound engineering – especially to newcomers – so I have dedicated a short chapter to them. I apologise if this chapter seems overly mathematical, but they were originally a way of dealing with the maths of long distance telephone systems. But if you don't get the maths don't worry about it, just keep the concepts in mind and the maths often comes later.

I recently came across a question in a well-known UK game show: "What is the unit Decibel associated with?" The 'correct answer' given by the question master was, perhaps understandably, incorrect – "Sound Level". I say incorrect because decibels with no reference are simply a way of expressing a fraction such as ½ or ¼. If you say "decibels SPL" then you are explicitly referring to sound pressure level as the quiz question asked.

In order to clarify my ramblings, let's look at the history of the decibel. In the first quarter of the 20th century, losses in long distance telephone wires were measured in Miles of Standard Cable. This 'real world' system was a way of expressing the significant losses in terms of power received out of one end of a telephone line against power in at the other. In an amplifier we would expect this relationship to be greater than 1 – i.e. power out is greater than power in – the clue is in the name amplifier. An amplifier makes the signal bigger by amplifying it. On the other hand cables (especially long distance telephone cables) have loss and so lose power, so the relationship will be less than 1, so power out is less than power in. Long distance telephone lines had to have many repeater amplifiers to keep boosting the signal and counteract the cable losses. Keeping a track of these losses and gains means a lot of multiplication and division – which was very tiresome in the days before computers and calculators. Taking the logarithm of the values (using log tables) made the maths easier as multiplication is replaced by simple addition and division is replaced by subtraction.

Here's a quick explanation of what a logarithm (or Log) is. Take the example of multiplying a number by itself, that is, squaring it.

$$10 \times 10 = 10^2 = 100$$

Which in words is:

ten times ten is equal to ten squared which equals one hundred.

A logarithm (log) is simply a function which reverses this process. So $\text{Log}_{10}100 = 2$

Which in words is:

log (to the base ten) of one hundred is equal to 2.

We only need concern ourselves with base 10 and so the subscript 10 is often omitted thus $\text{Log}\ 100 = 2$.

So expanding this principle to more powers of ten

$10^2 = 10\times10 = 100$	$\text{Log}_{10}100 = 2$
$10^3 = 10\times10\times10 = 1000$	$\text{Log}_{10}1000 = 3$
$10^4 = 10\times10\times10\times10 = 10,000$	$\text{Log}_{10}10,1000 = 4$
$10^5 = 10\times10\times10\times10\times10 = 100,000$	$\text{Log}_{10}100,000 = 5$

I hope it is clear that a log function is used to find the power to which the base must be raised to in order to get the value specified. For example $10^3 = 1000$ so $\text{Log}_{10}1000 = 3$ and so on. It may get a little confusing when logs start returning value like 4.73 but don't worry about it – the principle is the same.

If we now start to apply this to our original discussion about telephone lines and booster amplifiers, the engineers took the ratio of power out (P_{out}) to power in (P_{in}) then expressed it as a fraction:

$$\frac{P_{out}}{P_{in}}$$

Then we can then take the Log_{10} of this and get

$$\log_{10}\frac{P_{out}}{P_{in}}$$

This is the formula to calculate bels, which are named after Alexander Graham Bell by engineers at Bell Labs in honour of their founder. In practice the bel was found to be rather a large unit for the job – in much the same way as a metre is a large unit for measuring everyday objects. So, in the same way as the centimetre (100th of a metre) became the everyday unit, so the decibel (10th of a bel) became common and the formula became:

$$dB = 10 \log_{10} \frac{P_{out}}{P_{in}}$$

This being 10 times the value of the bel formula.

It is important to note that any figure expressing a ratio of two identical units is a unit divided by another identical unit (in this case power/power) and so has no units of its own as they cancel out; it is simply a ratio and a value quoted in decibels is simply a ratio.

The decibel ratio is used to express ratios of power in losses and gains in electronic systems such as amplifiers and transmission lines and other systems. It is used by telephone engineers, sound engineers, video engineers, computer network engineers and any other people involved with moving electronic signals through wires, amplifiers and any other signal processing from mobile phones to medical scanners. In so doing the massive multiplication and division factors involved can be simplified to small easy to manage numbers that can be simply added together or subtracted. Consider this:

Power gain in dB	Power gain as a multiplication
0	1
10	10
20	100
30	1000
40	10,000
50	100,000
60	1,000,000

Table 6.1 Power gain in dB and multiplication factor.

A fader on a typical mixing console will have a scale reading -50dB somewhere near the bottom, and +10 at the top, so that's a difference of 60dB. This corresponds to a gain factor of one million (x 1,000,000). So pushing that fader from near the bottom to the top is asking your audio system to increase its output by a million times. So you can see in this simple example that the simple request "can you turn that up by 20dB?"

is much simpler than "can you increase the power output by a factor of a hundred?".

It is worth mentioning that we can (and often do) use decibels to compare voltages and currents too. But there is one complication in doing so – remember (chapter 4) that P=V²/R (power equals voltage squared divided by resistance). This means that the formula for dealing with decibels in reference to voltage (and current) is slightly different:

$$dB = 20\,\log_{10}\frac{V_{out}}{V_{in}} \qquad \text{or} \qquad dB = 20\,\log_{10}\frac{I_{out}}{I_{in}}$$

where V is voltage and I is current.

Fixed Reference decibels

Having said that decibels are simply a way of expressing a ratio and so have no absolute value, there are a few examples of 'fixed value' decibels where the in parameter is given a specific and fixed reference value. In such cases a suffix of one or more letters is used. Table 6.2 gives some common examples:

Convention	Meaning	Formula
dBm	Power relative to 1mW	$dB = 10\,\log_{10}\dfrac{P[watts]}{0.001[watt]}$
dBV	Voltage relative to 1V	$dB = 20\,\log_{10}\dfrac{V[volts]}{1[volt]}$
dBu	Voltage relative to 0.775V	$dB = 20\,\log_{10}\dfrac{V}{0.775[volts]}$
dB$_{spl}$	Sound Pressure Level relative to 20µPa	$dB = 20\,\log_{10}\dfrac{p[pascals]}{20[micro\ pascals]}$

Table. 6.2 Common fixed references for decibels.

I have shown the units in [square brackets], for these values to be correct these must be the units used.

Some of these 'reference values' might seem a little odd but there are reasons. For example dBu is referenced to 0.775V (or 775mV as you might see it written). At first this seems like a very odd number to choose, but it is the voltage required to drive 1mW into an impedance of 600Ω.

This again dates back to telephone systems. In modern electronics where low impedance transistor outputs (albeit in integrated circuits) can easily drive several high impedance inputs, fewer transformers are used on input and output stages (if at all) and there is usually no need to consider 'line impedance' in the same way as was necessary in the past with transformer outputs on valve amplifiers[1] where source impedance had to match load impedance. So the dBu has become the most common 'absolute' decibel and you will usually see meters calibrated in dBu. Table 6.3 gives some examples:

Voltage	Formula	dBu
0.775V	$20 \log_{10} \dfrac{0.775}{0.775}$	0dBu
10V	$20 \log_{10} \dfrac{10}{0.775}$	22.2dBu
0.1V	$20 \log_{10} \dfrac{0.1}{0.775}$	-17.8dBu

Table. 6.3 Voltage values to dBu.

Note that values below 0.775 are negative and those above are positive; this is how Logs work.

To convert dBu into volts you need the reverse function as shown in table 6.4.

---

1   Valve (or tube) amplifiers that were used in the days before transistors, had to use input and output transformers as the anode voltage was at least 100V and sometimes much higher. So the output voltage without a transformer would be a significant fraction of this and the input stage 'floats' at around this value. Clearly, having these sorts of voltages around in studios was undesirable. And the output had to be reduced and this large DC component removed before you could feed a load like a loudspeaker. Also early transistor amplifiers had very low input impedances that frequently needed to be altered to suit the application and transformers were a relatively simple way of doing this. As electronics has evolved the need for transformer coupling has diminished as electronic input and output stages are much cheaper (and lighter) to manufacture. That said there are still valid reasons for choosing transformer coupling and so manufacturers often offer it as an option especially on higher cost equipment.

dBu	Formula	Voltage
0dBu	$0.775 \times 10^{(0/20)}$	0.775V
22.2dBu	$0.775 \times 10^{(22.2/20)}$	10V
-17.8dBu	$0.775 \times 10^{(-17.8/20)}$	0.1V

Table. 6.4 dBu values to voltage.

Sound Pressure Level

The reference value for sound pressure level, dB_{spl} is 20µPa (20 micro pascals). We looked at this value in chapter 2, and it is the quietest pressure variation that an average healthy young adult ear can hear and the movement created by it moves the ear-drum by a distance equivalent to diameter of an atom! To convert pressure change in Pascals to dB_{spl} we use a similar method to those for voltage as shown in table 6.5

Pressure Change	Formula	dB_{spl}
20µPa 0.00002Pa	$20 \log_{10} \dfrac{0.00002}{0.00002}$	$0dB_{spl}$
1mPa 0.001Pa	$20 \log_{10} \dfrac{0.001}{0.00002}$	$34dB_{spl}$
0.1Pa	$20 \log_{10} \dfrac{0.1}{0.00002}$	$74dB_{spl}$

Table. 6.5 Pressure to dB_{spl}.

It is important to realise that sound pressure is to sound power what voltage is to electronic power so we use the 20Log formula for dB_{spl} as we do for voltage and current.

Converting dB_{spl} to actual pressure change is also similar as shown in fig. 6.6.

You will often see dBA, and dBC in relation to sound pressure level. In this case a correction curve has been incorporated into the measurement in order to mimic the non-linear response of the human ear.

dB_{spl}	Formula	Pressure Change
$0\ dB_{spl}$	$0.00002 \times 10^{(0/20)}$	0.00002Pa
$34\ dB_{spl}$	$0.00002 \times 10^{(34/20)}$	0.001Pa or 1mPa
$74\ dB_{spl}$	$0.00002 \times 10^{(74/20)}$	0.1Pa

Table 6.6 dB_{spl} to Pressure.

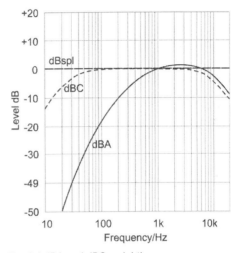

Fig. 6.1 dBA and dBC weighting curves.

The base reference of dBA and dBC is still 20µPa but as you can see from the graph in fig 6.1, dBA severely attenuates the levels the effect of low frequencies in the measurement. This is because at lower listening levels the ear is much less sensitive to these frequencies and the measurement curve is set to reflect this. Historically there was also a dBB curve which lies between the 'A' curve and the 'C' curve but it was found that this wasn't very useful and so now we tend to just use the A, B and flat (dB_{spl}) curves. In addition there are other specialist dB weighting curves which are outside the scope of this book.

If you take a sound pressure reading of a music event with considerable low frequency energy, you will see that the dBC or dB_{spl} reading is a few dB higher than the dBA reading. The exact difference will depend on how much low frequency energy there is which is usually determined by the type of music[2].

Coming back to the quiz question we saw at the beginning of the chapter we can see that to say that 'Decibels are a unit of measurement of sound level' is clearly wrong. They can be used in that context, but they are used for so much more and these uses are far more common;

---

2   If you are constrained by an environmental noise limit at an event always check which (if any) weighting curves are specified; a noise limit of 90dBA will almost certainly be louder than 90 dBspl (flat).

in fact I have a widget on my mobile phone that gives me the signal strength that the phone is receiving from the local cell mast in dBm. At the moment it reads -95dBm which is a minute 0.3pW (0.3 pico watts or 0.3 x10^{-12}W or 0.000 000 000 000 003 Watts), but it isn't making any noise at all, thankfully!

Where this all gets very elegant is that if you push the fader on your mixing console up by 10dB then whatever that fader is controlling will get 10dB louder:

If that fader is an output, then providing that you're not driving a limiter or other dynamic device too hard and providing that you have the system headroom[3] to do it, then the sound from the loudspeaker(s) connected to that output will get 10dB louder and this could be measured by a sound pressure meter in front of those loudspeaker(s).

On the other hand, if that fader is an input channel, then the source it controls (a guitar or a flute for example) will get 10dB louder in the mix. Whether this produces a measurable change in overall output depends on what else is going on.

The other neat thing and perhaps their reason for existence is that if you have (for example) a pre-amplifier with 20dB gain and a line amp amplifier of 10dB gain and an attenuator of 3dB (-3dB gain, losses are always shown as negative) then your total system gain is simply 27dB:

$$20 + 10 - 3 = 27dB$$

Compare this to the 'linear method'. Taking the same example for: a pre amp with a gain of x100, a line amplifier with a gain of x10 and an attenuator with a loss of x½, your system gain is x500:

$$100 \times 10 \times \tfrac{1}{2} = 500. \text{ Which is easier?}$$

So to recap there are two basic forms of decibels: absolute and relative.

Relative is used to express a gain (or loss if negative) in a system, for example the gain of an amplifier is 32dB. These decibels are a 'dimensionless' unit that are used to describe the ratio by which something is made bigger or smaller. In most cases this will be a sound pressure level or a voltage in the signal chain.

Absolute is used to express a value relative to a known and fixed reference value such as the desk output is 12dBu or the sound in the room is 76dB$_{spl}$, although this expression is still based on the ratio principle.

---

3 Headroom is a term used to describe how close to your limit you are running. So if you run out of headroom something in your signal chain will start to distort (or clip) or worse tear itself to pieces, in the case of a loudspeaker cone!

7 SPECIFYING A LOUDSPEAKER REINFORCEMENT SYSTEM

It doesn't matter if you're designing a system for a music festival with an audience of 20,000 people, a musical theatre piece with live performers on trapeze playing bagpipes or a small lecture for less than a hundred people, the essential process is identical. Of course there are different considerations for music, speech, concerts and theatre. The economics of a situation often dictate the necessity to attempt to fit a given system to a particular application whereas the design ideal should be to select a system for a given situation based on a required specification.

The term 'sound system design' is a rather grand title for what every sound engineer in the field of live event must do at some point – often without even realising it. Some people get to make a career out of specialising in 'sound system design' be they technical advisers working for loudspeaker manufacturers whose job it is to help people select and use the appropriate products from their range or theatre sound designers who specify the appropriate equipment for a large musical show or other event. At the other end of the scale is the person who turns up at a gig with a truck full of 'what was available in the warehouse' and has to get that show up and running in the next few hours whilst also mixing the show and ringing ahead to book the crew accommodation for the next night; that person is also a sound system designer – he or she has to make precise judgements as to how to best utilise the available equipment in the venue that has to house the event in the time available.

In the next few chapters I will be breaking down the 'sound system' into three distinct parts:

- the loudspeakers
- the microphones and other sources
- the rest

In order to design an effective system we must consider:

- the position of the ears of each and every person we are providing for
- any back ground noise level that we need to exceed
- the acoustic nature of the room
- our potential 'gain before feedback' – when using microphones and loudspeakers in the same room

- noise exposure for audience and staff
- environmental limits imposed

Like any design process there will be some compromises to be made: availability of equipment, financial limits, time restrictions, physical restrictions of access or weight loading restrictions on supporting structures. The best design will be the one that manages these compromises in the best way and delivers the best possible result.

Some key design questions are:

Do I need a sound system and if so what type?

This may sound like a daft question but all too often the requirement for sound reinforcement is assumed. A small play in a small theatre is not likely to need any amplification – however there might be special circumstances to consider such as a noisy audience of excited children or that the venue is a tent that gets very noisy when it rains or some other source of high background noise. Perhaps the show has loud passages of music or sound effects that cause temporary threshold shift in the audience (i.e. their ears become less sensitive for a short period of time – this would require very careful handling by the operator). It is vitally important to get all of the information about the job you are being asked to do and leave nothing (or as little as possible) to chance.

What are actually going to use the sound system for?

If it is just speech then we needn't worry about the low frequencies too much: the deepest male voices only go down to about 120Hz and female down to about 200Hz. And these low frequencies contribute very little to actual intelligibility; in fact most vocal intelligibility is contained in the 600Hz to 8kHz region. Low frequency loudspeakers or (sub)woofers are usually large, heavy and take considerable amplifier power (which usually comes in large, heavy boxes and heavy with cables to match) so if we don't need them we can save a lot of time effort and money by not using them.

On the other hand if we need to produce exciting high quality music or soundscapes then we need to consider where these large low frequency loudspeakers can be sited to best complement the smaller mid and high frequency loudspeakers and some negotiation is usually required with those persons in charge of aesthetics. For example you might not get away with the 'ideal' position for your loudspeakers because they are (usually) large black boxes which might obscure the audience's view.

Where is the event to be situated?

This will have an effect on the background noise, the room acoustics and whether we need to consider weather-proof loudspeakers and other equipment. Outside events typically require more powerful systems as there is no reverberant field which has the effect of 'slowing the loss of energy' and increasing the level for the audience; outdoor situations are effectively anechoic.

How many people?

More people will normally require a 'bigger' system – at least in terms of acoustic output. But other factors will have an effect too: irregular shaped venues may call for a bias of power to compensate for longer distances to some sections of the audience. Additional subsidiary systems may be needed to cover areas around corners or just too far away to for the main system to cover.

Do we have live musicians? Do we have pre-recorded material?

Generally speaking the specification of a 'replay' only system is much easier than one which needs to handle live reinforcement as the feedback problem tends to be irrelevant (unless you're using vinyl for your source media).

How big is the stage (if there is one)?

If a performers' monitoring system is needed then the size of the stage and locations of the monitor speakers need to be considered. The physical dimensions will also dictate where a 'main' system can be positioned and the relative position of the loudspeakers and the sources has a big effect on the imaging – or perceived position of the sources. Is the stage a simple end-on arrangement or does it come out into the audience (thrust) or are the audience on all sides (in-the-round)? These different arrangements have a big effect on how the loudspeaker system is arranged and how its performance needs to be managed.

Is there more than one stage?

Music and theatre festivals might have different stages all around a central area, in which case care must be taken to minimise the effect one stage has on the audience of another. This problem can also exist if multiple stages exist within the same building. Less often but still possible is that a single event may use different 'stages' within the same performance as attention shifts from to another. In this instance the loudspeaker system needs to ensure the focus is always directed to the correct performance area.

Are we showing and video or film with special requirements such as 5.1 (or higher) surround sound?

Such systems can have quite carefully written guidelines as to how the reproduction system is to perform with a given space.

Specifying the Loudspeaker System

So let's make a start by considering a simple system for high quality speech reinforcement that might be used in environments such as theatres, conference venues, churches, meeting rooms etc. This system is probably the most common design but I'm sure it won't take you very long to find one that is done very badly! Perhaps the biggest practical question is – how 'big' does our sound system need to be?

For an absolute minimum our system needs to generate 6dB above the ambient level. However, this is supermarket PA standard – be heard but only just. Far better is to aim for at least 10dB above ambient. Ideally give yourself 25dB of headroom which is the maximum useful amount and so it is very much an ideal. That said, it is important to realise that background levels can and will fluctuate – if you design your system to only provide 10dB headroom and your background noise goes up by 8dB then you have less than the absolute minimum to play with and you've lost! Aiming for 25dB above you anticipated upper level of background gives you some scope if you've underestimated. If you know the background will rise above this then aim higher still and take your headroom above what you think your maximum background level.

So by applying the inverse square law (assuming that we're in the direct field) then taking the distance from the loudspeaker to the listener we can calculate what level the loudspeaker needs to produce. Here's an example: consider a room with an ambient noise level of 55dBspl – such as a theatre with some air handling or fan noise from luminaires or projectors.

So let's aim for a target SPL 25dB above this which gives us a target spl of 55+25 = 80dBspl.

Then let's consider a distance from listener to loudspeaker of 20m. According to the inverse square law this distance corresponds to an spl reduction $20 \times \log_{10} 20 = 26$dB.

So to be effective according to our first design spec, we need the loudspeaker to produce = 80 + 26 = 106dBspl.

If we want to add some more headroom to allow for some natural speech dynamics then we can add 12dB here. So we can aim to produce 118dB spl. For music we'd push this a little higher – maybe to 18dB.

Now we need to look at our loudspeaker options. Some manufacturers produce matched loudspeaker/amplifier-controller systems, either with dedicated external amplifier-controller units or the amplifier-controllers built into the loudspeaker cabinet. In this context amplifier-controller refers to an electronic system which not only acts as a power amplifier but also handle the necessary frequency band division (crossover), frequency corrections (equalisation), phase and time correction (time-alignment) and most importantly, driver protection (limiting). For more on this see the next chapter.

This approach of managing the loudspeaker allows manufacturers to specify a maximum spl to which the matched amplifier/loudspeaker system can reliably achieve and you don't have to do any more work!

An example is given in table 7.1 which gives us pretty much all of the information that we require: the maximum practical sound pressure level (spl), the frequency response, the dispersion angles, the size and the weight. The spl we require is at least 118dB so this example which gives us 123dB is ideal.

Components	6.5" driver / 1" compression driver with CD horn
Max. sound pressure (1m, free field) with specified amplifier	123 dB SPL
Frequency response (-5 dB)	85Hz - 20 kHz
Nominal dispersion angle (h x v)	100° x 55°
Dimensions mm (h x w x d)	300 x 188 x 175
Weight kg	5

Table 7.1 Example specification for a small loudspeaker from a manufacturer of matched loudspeaker/amplifier-controller systems.

The size and weight are also very important and yet are an often overlooked aspect of a loudspeaker. Having a loudspeaker that performs better than any other in all aspects (spl delivery, frequency response and sound quality) is completely useless if it is too big and heavy to get into the correct location for the job; better results are usually achieved by getting an 'average' loudspeaker in the right place over getting a 'perfect' loudspeaker in the wrong place. We will look at what constitutes the 'right' and 'wrong' places later in this chapter.

On the other hand, some manufacturers use a different design concept and give information with which you can specify the preferred amplifier with which to drive the loudspeaker. An example is given in table 7.2.

In this case we have a little more work to do to get to our target spl value. We need to start with the sensitivity value. This tells us how much spl the unit generates per unit of power applied, so we can relate this to the maximum power handling with this formula:

$$dB_{spl} = S + 10log_{10}P_{max}$$

Where dB_{spl} is maximum spl, S is sensitivity and P_{max} is maximum power handling. I know this formula looks a bit daunting but in footnote(1) I have shown how to create a little spread-sheet to work it out for you[1]. It simply takes the maximum power (referenced to 1 watt) and turns it into decibels, then adds the sensitivity to find the maximum spl.

This example gives us a calculated maximum spl of 124dB provided that we use an amplifier that can provide at least 400W of power. In practice a little headroom in the amplifier is always a good idea as we are less likely to overdrive it. Manufacturers will often provide a recommended amplifier power which usually adds 3dB or so to the rated power, which in this case would mean an amplifier of about 600W would be suitable.

Components	LF 300mm / 75mm voice coil & 25mm exit HF compression driver
Rated Power	400W
Sensitivity (1W @ 1m)	98dB
Recommended Amplifier	400-600W into 8 ohms
Frequency Response (± 3dB)	70Hz-18kHz (-10dB @ 52Hz)
Nominal impedance	8 ohms
Dispersion (h x v -6dB)	60° x 40°
Dimensions mm (h x w x d)	555 x 365 x x 365
Weight kg	24.5

Table 7.2 Example specification for a loudspeaker where any amplifier can be used.

Whichever option we choose for our basic system, we have a system capable of producing sound pressure levels that have the potential to damage hearing, so we need to be careful not to expose some of our

1   For those of you comfortable with formulae in spread sheets, make cell A1 your sensitivity (1W 1m), make cell A2 your maximum power handling in watts and your formula for your spl cell is this: = A1 + 10*LOG10(A2)

audience to such high sound levels in order to achieve our desire goal elsewhere in the audience.

For Best Results Point the Loudspeakers at the Listeners!

This may sound like the most obvious statement imaginable, but I'm guessing that it won't take you too long to find a system where the installers have failed at this basic task and fixed some loudspeakers flat against a wall firing straight over the heads of the people who supposed to be hearing them.

Loudspeakers are a bit like spotlights. Actually they're more like PAR cans[2] with an asymmetric beam and an edge to that beam that isn't a well-defined sharp cut-off, but hopefully you can see what I'm saying; most of the useful energy comes straight out of the front of the device in a direction (usually) perpendicular[3] to the baffle. Spotlights (and PAR cans) have the job of controlling a frequency band of light of less than 1 octave and at wavelengths that are minute (hundreds of billionths of a metre) as we saw in chapter 2. These wavelengths are minute in comparison to the device being used to generate and control them. As such they do a very easy job of gathering up all the light and throwing it out in one direction with almost perfect control. On the other hand even small loudspeakers that are band limited to 100Hz to 16kHz are tasked with producing and controlling over 6 octaves which is a range of wavelengths from 3.4m to 2cm. There are very few devices in other fields of wave physics from huge radio telescopes, microwave ovens to TV aerials that have to deal with such a vast variation in wavelengths. This means that loudspeakers can never be 'perfect' devices; they will never be able to control their entire operating frequency range in a consistent and uniform way whilst at the same time being usable in real world applications. We need to be aware of these limitations when we are considering our loudspeaker system design specification.

So the next thing we need know from our manufacturer(s) is how our loudspeaker disperses the sound it produces. There are various terms for this including dispersion characteristics, directivity and directionality. This is a pretty complex field and the more drivers there are in the

---

2   The PAR in PAR can stands for Parabolic Aluminiumised Reflector. These are sealed-beam lamps where all the optics are sealed into a single unit. The can is just that a simple pressed metal shell which does little more than hold the sealed-beam lamp unit in place and offer a place to put the colour-filter frame. If you want a wide beam unit you buy a wide-beam lamp and for a narrow beam you buy a narrow-beam lamp. Modern miniature 12V MR16 down-lights are very similar.

3   Some loudspeakers have deliberately asymmetric dispersion patterns intended for specific applications – another reason to always check the manufacturer's specification before use.

loudspeaker and the less symmetrical their arrangement, the more complex it becomes. Consequently several methods have evolved for presenting concise versions of this complex data into a usable form. None of the methods shown here will give a truly exhaustive representation of the loudspeaker's behaviour but they should be enough for our purposes:

Simple numeric values

Both the example tables above quote a dispersion figure of horizontal beam angle by vertical beam angle (h x v), one being 100° x 55°, the other being 60° x 40°. These are nominal values and give you a guide as to how the much 'area' the loudspeaker is designed to cover. If you imagine the sound energy radiating from the front of the loudspeaker in a simple elliptical cone shape, then these figures define the edges of that cone as shown in fig. 7.1.

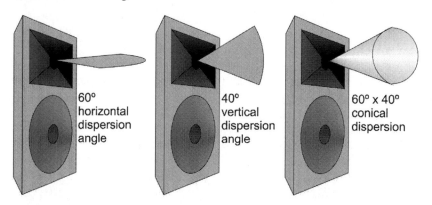

Fig. 7.1 Simple Dispersion Angle.

Polar Plot

Polar plots are simply circular graphs that show how much the output of the loudspeaker reduces as you move away from the centre axis. By producing different plots for different frequencies and for horizontal and vertical planes a much better picture of the loudspeaker's behaviour can be achieved.

Looking at the polar plot in fig 7.2, which is measured at 1kHz, the 'straight ahead' main axis is shown at the top of the diagram (0°), with the red line showing horizontal dispersion and the blue line vertical. Each radial (outwards from centre) line is 10° either to the left or right (horizontal) or above and below (vertical) of centre and each concentric (ring) line is 5dB; I have flagged two points, one in vertical plane and one in the horizontal.

The horizontal one shows that, at the specified frequency, the output falls gradually as you move away from the centre line and when you're 50° off the main axis, the output will be 5dB lower than straight ahead. Beyond this, the output falls away quite rapidly:

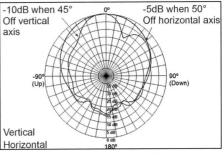

Fig. 7.2 Example Polar Plot showing horizontal and vertical dispersion.

-5dB @ 50°, -10dB @ 80°, -15dB @ 110°,-20dB @ 160° beyond this a small lobe pushes the output back up to -15dB @ 180.

This plot is from a loudspeaker that has a horn/compression-driver assembly centrally mounted above a central 12" driver like the one shown in the simple dispersion cone diagram fig 7.1. The cabinet is physically symmetrical from left to right and this is reflected in the left-right symmetry of the red (horizontal line) in the polar plot.

The vertical (blue) line shows that, at the specified frequency, the output falls more sharply to -10dB at only 45° off axis when moving upwards. The loudspeaker is not vertically symmetrical and, as you might expect, neither is its behaviour and this is reflected in the polar plot. For this loudspeaker (and for many) the frequency of 1kHz is right in the middle of the crossover region where both the HF horn and the LF driver are working together. This forms complex interactions and leads to these irregularities in the dispersion characteristics. Looking at the 45° downwards angle (right hand side) you can see that the level is only 5dB lower, having dipped below -10dB at 20°. These complexities are very common and different things happen at different frequencies; now you can see why just saying 60°horizontal x 40°vertical is a considerable over-simplification.

Polar plots are probably the most universal way of presenting useful data about loudspeakers but they are rather unwieldy; to be readable the most you can get onto a single plot is a single frequency horizontal and vertical graph, and then to be truly representative you need at least 1/3 octave resolution – so for 100Hz to 20kHz (just under 8 octaves) you need 23 plots. You can put several bands onto one plot using colours or different dotted line types but this makes it harder to read.

Beamwidth Graphs

Beamwidth graphs show how the actual width of the horizontal and vertical dispersion angles vary with frequency: frequency is shown along the horizontal (x) axis and beamwidth in degrees is up the vertical (y) axis. So for any frequency you read off the angle of the vertical and horizontal beam. This provides a more accurate version of the simple 60° x 40° figure that we started with. One of the problems with them is that they don't tell you how the beam varies up or down or side to side – only that it gets wider or narrower in a given plane; as we seen with the polar plots, the variation can be very asymmetric and this asymmetry is not shown in this type of plot.

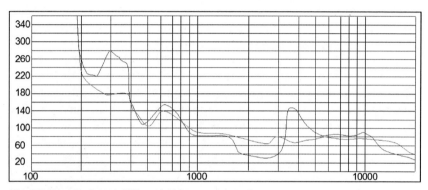

Fig. 7.3 Example beamwidth against frequency graph.

Isobar Plots

Isobar plots are probably the most concise way of presenting useful data in a way that's relatively quick and easy to digest, once you know how to read them. Like the beamwidth plots the horizontal (x) axis represents frequency and the vertical (y) axis is the beam angle. They key difference is that the plot is arranged around the central 0° reference which refers to the line straight ahead of the loudspeaker – like the top of the polar plot we looked at before. So, for the vertical plot everything above this 0° line shows what happens as we move above the loudspeaker and everything below it show what happens when we move below the loudspeaker. Similarly for the horizontal plot the area above the 0° line typically shows what happens to the left of the cabinet and the area below show what happens to the right – though check this with the manufacturer if the plot doesn't explicitly state this. Fig. 7.4 shows a loudspeaker plot for the vertical dispersion, while Fig 7.5 shows the same loudspeaker's horizontal behaviour.

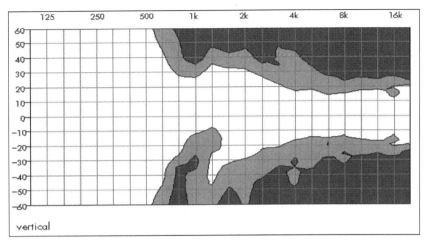

Fig. 7.4 Vertical isobar plot of frequency against dispersion.

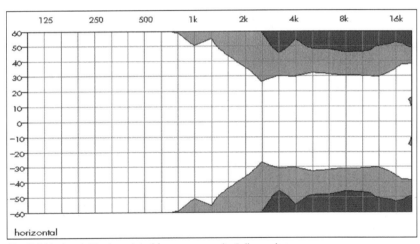

Fig. 7.5 Horizontal isobar plot of frequency against dispersion.

These isobars plot show a typical narrowing of the dispersion in the horizontal plane once we get below about 800Hz, with a very typical slight widening between 1kHz and 1.2kHz then constant narrowing down to around 3kHz. The slight widening is caused by the interaction between the 12" LF driver and the horn assembly through the crossover region where these two dissimilar systems share the work. This kind of detail is much more difficult to spot in a polar plot.

When we look at the vertical polar plot (fig. 7.4) we can see something strange in the downward direction happening between 800Hz and 3kHz. Here, again through the crossover region where the LF and HF drivers are working together, we can see a downward 'lobe' develop which peaks at about 1.2kHz and widens out to 45° before it comes under control beyond 2kHz and mirrors the upwards dispersion thereafter. We can see this on the polar plot too although, again, it can be harder to see the extent of this.

Most 12" and horn loudspeakers will exhibit some anomalies like these through the crossover frequencies as the physical spacing of the drivers causes interference lobes through their shared range of frequencies. For this reason it is important to be able to see them in the data so that you can best choose how to avoid potential problems. For instance the particular example shown here has lead many designers to hang this particular cabinet upside-down when used over the centre stage so that this lobe was aimed up and away from the stage area where performers were using omni-directional head-worn radio microphones, and thus helped reduce feedback problems in the 1.2kHz region – which as we have seen is a vital frequency range for intelligibility.

Perhaps, what started out as a blindingly obvious statement, *for best results point the loudspeakers at the listeners* doesn't seem quite so simple now. But we have looked at the data necessary to decide how to point the loudspeakers at the listeners based on how the energy radiates from the front of the loudspeaker. From this information we can decide what choices of loudspeaker to make and how to position them to cover the area in which the listeners will be situated.

Audience Area

The next consideration is where those listeners will be. In an ideal world we will always have the time, information and budget to make informed choices based on freely available and accurate information relating to all aspects of the 'show', the venue and the listeners. Back in the real world we will all have, or have had occasions when we roll up to a venue we've never seen before with a show we don't know enough about with a truck load of gear specified by somebody else and be expected to make it work! Wherever we fit on this scale of idealism, all the principles of correct loudspeaker specification and positioning will make the end result better and our job easier. For the time being let's assume that we have some clear idea as to the shape and size of the listener-area.

We have already seen how we can estimate the necessary spl for a given situation, based simply on a target value and the inverse square law. Next we need to:

- Ensure that everybody gets some direct sound.

(so we need to)

- Point the loudspeakers in the right direction.
- Avoid obstructions between the listeners and the loudspeakers.
- Maximise the direct to diffuse ratio for as much of the audience as possible.
- Not have some areas too loud whilst others are too quiet (even coverage).
- Take care over workers' exposure – we are all bound by noise at work regulations. Some occasions will also dictate that the audience is bound by some noise limits too. Whilst these are usually based on noise-at-work values the exact nature of the restriction will depend on the event, location and the licensing authority.
- We might also need to consider the transmission of the 'noise' that we generate to other people who are neither performers, employees or audience. They might be other people working or living in the same building or even adjacent buildings. Our beautiful event is somebody else's noise!

So coming back to where we started from with a need to generate 106dBspl and cover a small audience, let's make this into a more real-world situation.

This could be a presentation based on the spoken word which is actually one of the hardest things to get 'right'. Or it could be a singer in a small venue.

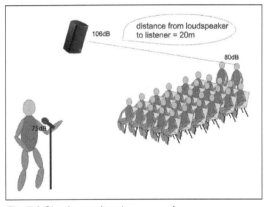

Fig. 7.6 Simple vocal system example.

But if we can successfully reproduce the details of the high speech/song intelligibility then we have a good system that we can use as the basis for other functions.

- We had a room with an ambient noise level of 55dBSPL
- We were aiming for a target SPL 25dB above this: Target spl level (55+25) = 80dBSPL.

- We had a distance from farthest listener to loudspeaker of 20m which corresponds to an spl reduction 20 x $\log_{10} 20$ = 26dB.
- So we needed the loudspeaker to produce = 80 + 26 = 106dBSPL.

We added some more headroom to allow for some natural speech/ music dynamics so we added 12dB here. So we can aim to produce 118dB SPL.

Just a note about headroom – headroom is great, the more you have the louder your system will go before it starts to distort, so you should always aim to have a reasonable amount on tap. But headroom costs money and headroom adds weight; to have plenty of headroom you need to 'overspec' your system which usually means bigger, more powerful loudspeakers which require bigger more powerful amplifiers to drive them, and this usually means more cabling, more rigging, etc. To add 6dB you need amplifiers that are four times more powerful and loudspeakers to cope with that power.

For more dynamic music you'll probably need 16 or even 20dB of headroom. Personally I like to know that, if I have set up my system to provide that 20dB of headroom then my 'running level' has the console meters running at 0dB, so I know I have optimised the system, as best as I can. Most consoles give you between 12dB and 18dB above that 0dB and I want to know that it is available if I need it. But it can be costly to do.

Fitting the Loudspeakers into the Space

Now we can look at how we use the directional data in terms of how the loudspeaker coverage patterns look in the context of a plan of the room. It is always best to work with as much information as possible and wherever possible you should attempt to get accurate drawings for any venues you do not know.

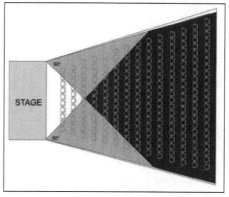

Fig 7.7 shows an example of a simple fan-shaped auditorium with a single loudspeaker either side of the stage; the overlapping area is shaded darker. If we use 60°units we get good pattern control, keeping most of the energy away from the side walls, but we have a

Fig 7.7 End-on stage with fan shaped auditorium, using two 60° loudspeakers with a coverage gap in the front few rows.

distinct hole in the middle of the front two rows.

Using two 90° cabinets we fill in the hole but we have a much larger amount of energy hitting the side walls as shown in fig. 7.8. This energy will most likely reflect and increase our reverberant field. As we saw in Chapter 5 this can have a detrimental effect on our event as we will inevitably decrease the ratio of direct to diffuse (reverberant) sound for a larger portion of our audience.

Another option is shown in fig. 7.9 using two 70° loudspeakers as before with a third front fill added to fill in the hole. This front fill need not be as loud as the main side speakers as it has far fewer people to address all of whom are far closer.

The ground-plan view is only part of the situation and cannot be taken in isolation; we also need to consider the section too.

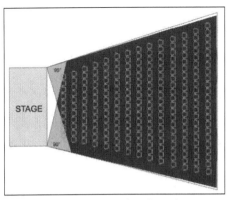

Fig 7.8 End-on stage with fan shaped auditorium using two 90°loudspeakers.

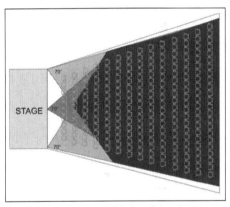

Fig. 7.9 End-on stage with fan shaped auditorium using two 70° with a single front fill.

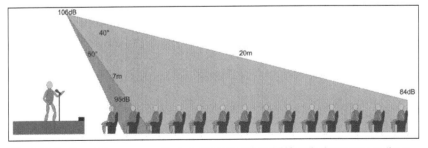

Fig. 7.10 Section of the same auditorium showing 40° and 50°vertical coverage options flown at a height of 5m.

If we look at this section in fig. 7.10 which shows two options of loudspeaker flown at a height of 5m; one being 40° vertical, and one being 50° vertical. As we can see the 40° reaches the back row, with some allowance for anybody standing in the back isle, but at the expense of the front two rows. The 50° option just covers the front row so the front fill we looked at earlier would make an ideal combination. However if we now look at the relative levels as we move back away from the stage, the end of the front rows are hearing a potential 90dB (being 7m away from the main loudspeakers and using the $20 \times \text{Log}_{10}$ distance formula) whereas the back row are only hearing 80dB (20m from the loudspeaker) which is a variation of 10dB. This is worst case as the back row may well be into the reverberant field which as we have seen is a steady state over the inverse square law of the direct field. So the back row might, in reality, be a couple of dB louder thus reducing the variation to about 8dB but this is still quite a wide range. A far better target for variation throughout the room is 6dB and the best case is 3dB or less. So our basic design clearly has some flaws.

If we ground stack the system as in fig. 7.11 then the level variance problem becomes much worse. Here were using the same 40° loudspeaker but this time we have simply sat it on the stage or 'flown' it very low so that it the same height as the performer.

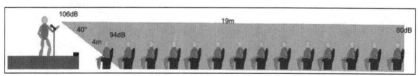

Fig. 7.11 Section of the same auditorium showing 40° vertical coverage ground stacked, or flown low.

The problems this generates are:

The loudspeaker is closer to the performer (see the section below on feedback) so our gain before feedback will be reduced

The front row is now much closer to the loudspeaker whereas the distance to the back row is very little different. This means that the front/back level variance is much worse (14dB) than it was with a system flown at 5m.

I hope that this demonstrated the huge advantage of 'flying' the loudspeaker system in that it allows best control of the coverage and evens the level distribution.

In the next chapter we look at how to use multiple loudspeakers in the form of clusters and delays to allow larger and more complex spaces to be covered. In addition these techniques allow each loudspeaker to work less hard and so, particularly for the loudspeakers close to the stage, we can improve our potential gain before feedback.

Chapter 9 has a more detailed look at how feedback occurs and how to manage it.

8 DELAYS, CLUSTERS AND ARRAYS

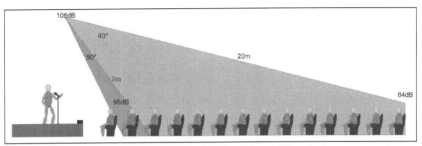

Fig. 8.1 Section of the sample auditorium showing 40° and 50°vertical coverage options flown at a height of 5m.

In the last chapter we had the situation shown above where we could achieve reasonable coverage and we were just within the limits of acceptable *gain before feedback* but we had a wide range of listening levels as we moved away from the stage towards the back of the room. So what happens if we put an additional set of loudspeakers half way down the room as shown in Fig. 8.2?

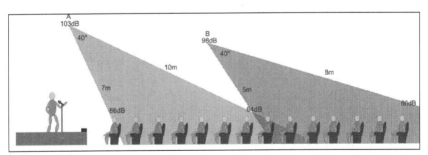

Fig. 8.2 Section of the auditorium with a primary 40° system flown at 5m, with a 'delay' system flown half way along the room.

In this case we still have our target SPL of 80dB at the rear of the audience, but now we have a range between the front and the back of only 6dB and we have reduced the main speaker level by 3dB so this will give us even more gain before feedback, by reducing the level of direct sound being heard on the stage.

There is one problem which we need to overcome: the electricity in the loudspeaker cable will travel at over half the speed of light[1] (at least 149 896 000 ms[-1]) while sound travels through the air at a much more pedestrian 343 ms[-1], this makes the electrical signal in the cable about five hundred thousand times faster than sound in air. So if we consider the area where the two loudspeakers overlap, the sound from loudspeaker (B) will arrive at the listener's ear in about half the time that the sound from loudspeaker (A) will arrive. The sound from (A) will take about 29ms and the sound from (B) will take only 15ms.

For those who want to work this out, this is how you'd do it. Remember the formula from chapter 2

$$t = {}^d/_s$$

Our distance from A is 10m so time = 10 / 343 which is about 0.029 seconds (29ms)

Our distance from B is 5m so time = 5 / 343 which is about 0.015 seconds (15ms)

Given that the sound from (B) will probably also be louder there are a few problems with this:

The listener will (by the precedence effect – see chapter 5) perceive the sound as coming from loudspeaker (B) and not from the stage.

There is a significant risk of loss of intelligibility as your listener hears the two arrivals. In larger venues or situations where the difference in arrival time exceeds 30ms then the risk of echo perception is highly likely.

When you listener is fed contradictory aural and visual images there is a very real tendency for the listener to lose concentration and have a much less satisfactory experience of the event.

Fortunately there is a very simple technique that can be applied to fix this multitude of problems – to add delay. This uses a device which literally delays the sound; anything coming into to a delay device will not simply appear at its output almost instantaneously, as you would expect of pretty much any other processing device in the signal chain. Instead you specify how long the device will 'hold' the signal for before releasing it. Such a *delay device* might be in any one of a number of places in the signal chain.

---

1   The actual speed of electricity in cables depends on the construction of the cable and specifically the insulation. In an open conductor the speed can be as high as 95% or more of the speed of light in a vacuum, in a co-axial cable it can be as low as 67%. Which is a range of between 194 865 098ms[-1] to 284 802 835ms[-1]. Either way it makes it pretty much instantaneous compared to the speed of sound in air.

It might be a stand-alone unit that is wired into the signal path before the amplifier that drives loudspeaker (B). In systems with analogue mixing consoles and analogue signal processing this is a very common solution and easy to add in.

It might be incorporated into the loudspeaker processor. This is common with higher end systems which have system controllers which are usually a combination of digital crossovers, equalisers, delays and limiters. Such devices are used to fine tune the loudspeaker performance (see next chapter) but often have some *spare* processing power that can be given over to user settings such as room equalisation and delay. Sometimes such facilities are actually built into the amplifier itself.

It might be available within a processor which incorporates equalisation, delay and other features.

It might be on the output of a digital mixing console.

Where ever this *delay* is applied it is there to compensate for the speed of sound in air over the speed of the electrical signal through the cabling and thus slow down the sound before it emerges out of loudspeaker (B). If, in the above instance, we apply 15ms of delay to the signal path feeding loudspeaker (B) then the arrival time of the sound from (A) and (B) will be much closer to the same value and, as we have seen in chapter 5, the ear-brain system is very capable of *merging* this into a single perceived sound. The closer the arrivals are together the easier it is for the ear-brain system to perform this remarkable task.

As we add more and more loudspeakers, like the front fill example we saw in the last chapter, then the situation becomes more and more complex. That said, we can apply the simple action of trying to keep all the arrival times with a narrow margin and working in a methodical and progressive way, away from the 'real' source then quite complex systems of multiple loudspeakers can be *time aligned* quite easily. The hardest thing is often getting enough time in the schedule to perform this task carefully and accurately as the process often requires a degree of reiteration – that is going back over loudspeakers that you have already done in order to check that settings are still valid as new loudspeakers are added to the system.

If we look at fig. 8.3 we see half of the auditorium we have been thinking about – I have only considered half because in a symmetrical space, the other half will be the same. I have taken just two sample listening positions and called them:

1. in the front row midway between the main PA and the front-fill on the centre line.

2. a couple of rows behind the line of delays, i.e. which they really start to work.

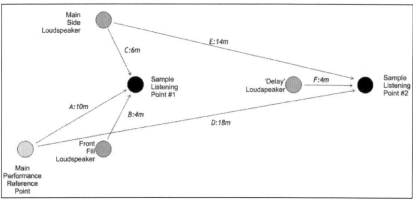

Fig. 8.3 Simple multi-point loudspeaker system for delay calculations.

I always find it much easier to start with time-zero at the front centre stage, or a little back from that where the main performer will be at least for the big numbers. So starting with listener #1 and using our time formula of

$$t = d/s$$

The sound has to travel 10m to reach #1 which is 0.029 seconds (29ms).

The sound from the front fill has to travel 4m to reach #1 which is 0.012 seconds (12ms).

The from the main loudspeaker has to travel 6m to reach #1 which is 0.017 seconds (17ms).

In order to make this work we need the first arrival to be 'A' from the natural stage sound.

So we add 0.02 seconds (20ms) delay to the front fill so that the actual arrival time at #1 is 0.02 (added delay time) + 0.012 (natural delay) = 0.032 seconds (32ms). This means that the sound from the front fill arrives very slightly after that from the stage but still well within our 30ms integration window (see chapter 5).

We then add 0.018 seconds (18ms) to the main loudspeaker system so that the actual arrival time at #1 is 0.018 (added delay time) + 0.017 (natural delay) = 0.035 seconds (35ms). Again this is slightly after both the sound from the front fill *and* the natural sound from stage. This should have the effect of clearly focusing the 'origin' of the sound as being the stage; the ear-brain system will perceive the sound from the main PA, even though it might be 10dB louder as that from front fill and stage, as being just a reflection and effectively ignore any directional information from it.

Then if we look at listening position #2 in a similar way:

The 'natural' sound has to travel 18m to reach #2 which is 0.052 seconds (52ms).

The sound from the main loudspeaker has to travel 14m to reach #2 which is 0.041 seconds (41ms) .

The sound from the delay speaker has to travel only 4m to reach #2 which is 0.012 (12ms).

So in order to make this work we need to add some delay to the loudspeakers again:

We have already added 0.018 seconds (18ms) to the main loudspeakers and this works here too. We now have 0.02 (added delay time) + 0.041 (natural delay) = 0.059 seconds (59ms).

We then add 0.05 seconds (50ms) to the delay loudspeaker which gives us 0.05 (added delay) + 0.012 (natural delay) = 0.062 seconds (62ms). Again this means that the delay loudspeaker 'lags' both the natural sound and that from the main loudspeaker and thus the ear-brain integrates this into the sound field and this delay loudspeaker should 'disappear' even though it is making considerable improvements in the quality of the experience.

The values I have chosen here may seem to have been plucked out of the air, but actually they are based on the difference between the arrivals (say path A and B which is 0.017 seconds) then I have added a few milliseconds (in this case rounded it up to 0.02 seconds) just to ensure that the natural sound arrives that bit sooner. In practice I find that this can be as much as 10ms (0.01 seconds) before it starts to get audible. The exact values will depend on the size of the venue and the complexity of your system. For any given listener you should aim to make the first arrival that of the natural sound. In a large auditorium as you move back away from the stage the natural sound becomes less important so the main loudspeakers can take over as your reference point. Then each loudspeaker that still lies in the direction of that natural sound becomes your next arrival and so on. Any arrivals that arrive outside the 30ms window will be heard as echoes and severely depreciate the sonic experience.

Arrays

So far I have only considered each loudspeaker as a single device that conforms to our requirements. In practice, especially as we need to increase the available sound pressure level (spl) groups of loudspeakers often called clusters or arrays become more important. Broadly these fall into two categories:

- Point-Source Arrays
- Line Arrays

Point-Source Arrays

With point-source arrays (which are often called clusters) individual loudspeakers are arranged in a group such that each member of that array 'covers' a certain section of the listening area. In this situation the ideal loudspeaker is one with a very tightly controlled 'beam' across its entire frequency range that focuses exactly on the area it is covering and nowhere else. In so doing, it avoids interference effects from neighbouring loudspeakers in the group; any one place in the audience will only be listening to the loudspeaker that is facing it. In addition the output beam must be as symmetrical as possible and originate from the centre point of the cabinet. Because each loudspeaker covers a relatively small area a given amount of power into the loudspeaker produces a louder SPL in that small area.

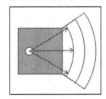

Fig. 8.4 Point source loudspeaker showing spherical wave-front from the constant distance from the 'acoustic centre'.

However to ensure no overlap these cabinets must be smaller than the shortest wavelength they are to reproduce and I hope it is clear from what you have read so far that this ideal is impossible to achieve: to have a single loudspeaker that can produce a controlled beam across the entire audio spectrum from a single point source would make the source less than 1cm across but the output aperture would need to be over 17m across.

Clearly this is a pretty impractical loudspeaker, so like all engineering solutions, the final *real world* solution will be some kind of compromise as we have seen in the previous chapter. Typically, a well-designed loudspeaker for arraying will have a high 'Q' so it will focus its beam accurately and beam will diminish rapidly off axis. The beam will be controlled for as wide a frequency range as possible and the various drivers will be closely spaced and may even be co-axial so that as much energy as possible radiates from the centre of the cabinet in a symmetrical manor. Fig. 8.4 shows a controlled conical dispersion like those we discussed in the previous chapter, in the frequency range in which the loudspeaker has good pattern control and the spherical wave-front radiates from the

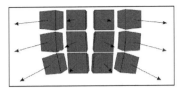

Fig. 8.5 Point source array.

acoustic centre of the cabinet. As the frequency goes down and wavelength increases, the directivity falls and the loudspeaker has less pattern control with less directivity. The cabinet and *flying* hardware will also be built in such a way as to allow the positioning of adjacent units as close as possible when the appropriate splay angle is used. The flying hardware is omitted from fig. 8.4 but you can see how the individual loudspeaker cabinets are arranged to focus on different areas of the audience.

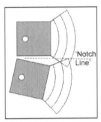

Fig. 8.6 Point source array showing comb-filter cancellation effects along the 'notch line'.

The main disadvantages of such arrays are:

Interference between cabinets which varies with the angle between them and leads to very noticeable comb-filter effects throughout the array's coverage. The extent of this varies with the cabinet design and flying arrangement and also the size of the array – the larger the array the more arrivals and the greater the time differences. Fig. 8.6 shows this effect in a simple two cabinet array but don't forget that these effects will occur in the vertical as well as horizontal lines between loudspeakers in the array and the more elements (loudspeakers) there are in the array, the more complex the situation becomes.

Line Arrays

A line array is relatively modern version of the column loudspeaker array which can trace its origins back to Harry Olson in 1957 and even beyond that back to Huygens wave theories in the 17th century. Column speakers were designed to control the vertical dispersion of vocal public address in order to improve intelligibility by limiting the excitation of the reverberant field – as we have discussed. This was achieved using closely spaced conventional drivers and was a very effective tool given the technology of the day. In fact you still see them in many ageing P.A. systems. However, it took some lateral thinking by a particle physicist in the 1980s by the name of Dr Christian Heil to adapt modern driver and waveguide technology to take this principle to a new level.

For wavelengths larger than the driver spacing, achieving a coherent column is relatively easy, the tricky part is doing the same with high power, high frequency drivers which produce wavelengths considerably shorter than the spacing between the drivers. Line array loudspeakers use various waveguide designs to produce a near flat wave-front in the high frequency range and then carefully designed flying hardware to close couple these wave-fronts so as to effectively approach an ideal flat wide band wave-front down the whole length of the array. As such the *line array* forms a single loudspeaker which has a customisable vertical coverage angle depending of the number of and angle between the individual loudspeaker elements used. The performance of any such line array can be predicted with the manufacturers' software prior to assembly. Given the time it takes to assemble and rig a line array and the number of variables available, it is essential that such prediction is done with as much accuracy as possible prior to starting the rigging process. In fact doing the simulation well in advance allows you to work out how many loudspeakers you need and so helps you plan your budget.

Fig. 8.7 shows how a wave guide is employed to lengthen the path between the high frequency driver and the front of the cabinet. This

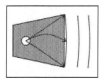

Fig. 8.7 Line source element showing wave guide effect to 'flatten' the wave-front.

makes the normally spherical wave-front much flatter which allows the high frequency to couple between adjacent array elements without the comb-filtering typical of point source arrays. The wave-front is not made completely flat to allow the lower section of the array to curve into the common 'J' shape as shown in fig. 8.8. This curvature allows the top of the array to close-couple into a tightly controlled long-throw array with a very narrow vertical dispersion, whilst the lower curved section progressively splays out to a wider vertical dispersion to cover the nearer listeners. Since there are fewer elements covering each area you get a natural reduction in SPL that usually follows the ideal design objective without need to use very much electronic compensation. The amount of splay you can put between the cabinets is defined by the curvature of the wave-front and so the dispersion angle of each cabinet.

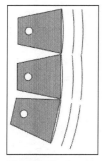

Fig. 8.8 Short 'J' shaped line array showing the flattened wave-front in action..

It is worth pointing out that a single line-array must be treated as a single loudspeaker. Never be tempted to send different signals to the top and bottom of the array as the whole principle will break down and become very unpredictable unless they have a single identical signal driving all elements.

Whilst there are some line array systems on the market which have variable horizontal dispersion, most are fixed. One common arrangement is that you have a choice of two horizontal widths (for example 70° and 120°), the wider is used at the bottom of the array to allow more coverage in the near-field audience area. See fig. 8.9.

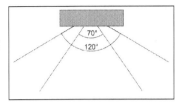

Fig 8.9 *Wider dispersion at the bottom of the array for near-field audience coverage.*

If you need more horizontal dispersion, then you need to hang line arrays side by side and then you have the interference patterns to consider all over again.

To Line or to Point – that is the Question

The question as to which type of array to use is a hotly contested topic; there are camps that refuse to employ line arrays for any application and some that only ever use line arrays even when they are clearly inappropriate.

My own take on the matter is that if you have relatively small systems in odd shaped rooms then a point source array will probably deliver better results. By small, I mean throws of around 40m or less. On the other hand even smaller but reverberant spaces are usually better served with careful line-array design to produce very tight pattern control and there are plenty of small format line array systems out there.

Don't forget that you don't have to plant yourself firmly in one camp or the other. You can use a line-array for you 'main system' and use single or small clusters of point source cabinets to fill-in the occasional gap. I would advise any readers to get as much information and training about the use of arrayed systems, be they line array or point source:

Look at the manufacturers' websites and see what the manuals and system design notes say.

- Do any on-line training course they might offer
- Attend hands-on training courses where possible

Most manufacturers are very keen to give training as it only serves their interests to make their products more accessible and to perform better if people know how to use them properly. This is important not just from an audio perspective but also from a safety point of view; large arrays can easily weigh several tonnes and knowing how to use the rigging hardware is vital if it is to be done safely.

9 FEEDBACK

In the live environment, feedback presents a big challenge. In this context I use the term feedback (as most live engineers do) to mean the nasty effect of having your amplified sound (from your loudspeakers picked up by your microphone(s) only to be further amplified into a continuous and

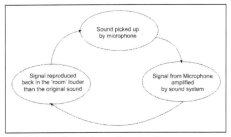

Fig 9.1 Feedback loop signal path.

self-sustaining loop. Broadcast and studio engineers sometimes use the term *howl*-round which is a nicely descriptive term. Feedback is very bad: it is painful to the listeners, it ruins the show and can even destroy equipment. Here's how it happens in our basic system.

Take this example:

The performer is generating 75dB measured at the microphone,

We raise this to 106dB at the loudspeaker in order to produce 80dB at the back of the room.

So we have added 31dB of 'gain' to the signal (75 + 31 = 106).

But we have a distance of 10m between the **microphone** and the loudspeaker.

Using our 20 x Log_{10} *distance* formula (20 x log_{10} 10 = 20) again we get a level drop of only 20dB over this distance.

So the microphone 'hears' the sound from the loudspeaker at 86dB which is 11dB louder than the original sound. When you add the 31dB of system gain this produces 117dB at the loudspeaker which is 11dB louder than the signal we started out with and the feedback loop is started as the sound gets louder and louder with each pass through the system.

So every sound entering the microphone is amplified and picked by the same microphone at a 11dB louder than it started out and on it goes until it reaches some physical limit. The only way to stop it is reduce the gain in the path of the loudspeaker – microphone – loudspeaker loop.

Good system design is the best way to reduce propensity to feedback by managing the relationship between loudspeaker coverage and microphone pick up pattern (see chapter 14) as well as looking at the

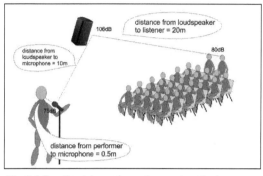

Fig. 9.2 Feedback loop shown in a real context.

potential system gain at the position of the microphone. But if we find that we have a feedback situation there are two ways to control it.

We can reduce the output of the loudspeaker close to the microphone, but this would reduce the level at the back of the room which was one of our design targets. So we would need to add some more loudspeakers closer to the back of the room to increase the level there.

We need to decrease the microphone-amplifier gain. But this would reduce the output from the loudspeakers which would probably compromise our system design still further. However, if we decrease the distance from the original sound source (in this case the performer's mouth) we will increase the level of this signal as it reaches the microphone by the inverse square law (an increase of 6dB for each halving of distance[1]). So if we measure 75dB at the microphone with it placed 0.5m from the performer's mouth then at 0.25m we will get 6dB more when we halve the distance (81dB) for no additional effort on the part of the performer. If we halve the distance again to 0.125m (a reasonable distance for a close mic'd singer) then we get another 6dB or 87dB.

Taking the second option first, with 87dB at the microphone we only need to introduce 19dB of gain to the signal chain to get 106dB from the loudspeaker. So we are below the 20dB that we need to avoid feedback – but only just.

Feedback Frequency Response

Feedback usually occurs at one or two specific frequencies for each given microphone. These frequencies correspond to peaks in the microphone-system frequency response at that point. Let's call this

---

1   Actually when we get very close to the source (mouth in this case) this principle breaks down as the microphone hears less than the entire mouth as it gets progressively closer. In this case this limit does not concern us as to get this close we would probably be choking the performer with the microphone and gain before feedback would cease to be the primary concern!

the *feedback frequency response* for the time being. It is important to appreciate that this doesn't mean the overall system response has this frequency response; this response that leads to feedback is caused by a combination of absorption, reflection, refraction and diffraction of the sound in the path between the loudspeaker and the microphone. In fact one important part of killing feedback is to find out *exactly* what the cause is. Ideally this needs to be done in a sound check when you can turn off specific loudspeakers to find which ones are causing your feedback – you will often find this surprising as I know I have. In a number of cases I have experienced the feedback has turned out to be from some small cheap self-powered loudspeaker that (for example) the keyboard player was using to take vocal cues from elsewhere the stage. The less-than-ideal frequency response of this unit coupled with a less-than well controlled dispersion pattern led to awful feedback that was so powerful it was assumed to be coming from the powerful side-fill stage monitors. So always spend a little time trying to find your feedback problem as you might find that moving a microphone or monitor can kill the problem without going to the last resort.

Controlling Feedback with Equalisation

As a last resort you can use equalisation (see chapter 13) to help manage feedback. I say as a last resort because now you are starting to affect the system performance. It is true that careful and gentle equalisation can really help you to control feedback, but you might be starting to affect the overall system frequency response for the worst if you are not careful.

That said, careful use of equalisation you can reduce the system gain at those specific frequencies to control the feedback. This technique is frequently used by monitor engineers whose very existence is to battle feedback on stage on a minute by minute basis. In addition theatre engineers who use radio microphones often find this technique essential as a final line in feedback control. The obvious problem with any moving microphone is that the *system frequency* response changes as the microphone moves around the sound field as the pattern of absorption, reflection, refraction and diffraction will change as the relationship between the microphone and the problem loudspeaker is changed. At the extreme you might even change the loudspeaker(s) that is (are) causing the problem as you move around.

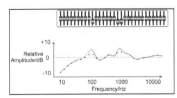

Fig. 9.3 Using a graphic equaliser to reduce feedback potential.

Fig. 9.3 shows the use of a graphic equaliser to reduce peaks in a system's feedback frequency response. The solid line shows the 'natural response' of a microphone-system and the dotted line shows the result affected by moving the graphic equaliser sliders shown at the top to reduce a number. The question is where to apply this equalisation.

If you apply it to the microphone, then every signal path fed by that microphone will be affected and that includes the audience, so you could compromise the sound the audience hears unnecessarily.

If you apply it to the loudspeaker that is causing the feedback then you are also affecting all the other sounds that emanate from that loudspeaker which might also compromise the sound unnecessarily.

The choice of where to apply the equalisation will depend entirely on the situation and is born out of experience.

Ringing

Ringing is the term used for the effect that often happens just before feedback takes off and becomes a real problem. It sounds like one or two frequencies that persist or *ring* for a little longer than they should. What happens is that there isn't quite enough system gain to self-sustain for the feedback to take hold, but there is enough to keep them going for a short time. With experience engineers can pick on this before anybody in the audience does and even before any performers do. If it suddenly starts when you push a particular fader up, then chances are it is the microphone on that channel that is the problem. In this case (especially if it during the main show) then it might be difficult to find the exact feedback path and the only option is to reach for the eq on that microphone channel to control the problem. Since that ringing will effectively amplify those frequencies for that microphone, then this is perfectly acceptable control method.

Beware Dynamic Processors

Just a final word on feedback when using dynamic processors. Beware any processors which **add** gain to the signal path such as expanders or gates (see chapter 13); these can catch out the inexperienced and experienced engineer alike.

Consider a gate set to open at particular signal level (threshold). When that gate is open it may well allow a channel with considerable gain to be activated. If that channel has enough gain to allow a feedback loop to be created and that feedback level is sufficient to keep the gate open, then there may suddenly be uncontrolled feedback when that gate opens.

10 MONITORS

Once we start to add sound reinforcement to a given environment we are by definition changing the characteristics of that environment. This means that the experience of the performers will be altered too and far from the room in which they rehearsed they now have a very different sounding space. In addition the demands of modern performances often dictate that performers are placed where they cannot hear each other. The solution to these and other similar problems is to use a stage monitor system.

So far we have only considered using loudspeakers to cover our audience, but here we have another application – to allow performers to hear themselves and others to create the sound field that they need to be able to perform. When we design stage monitor systems we need to use the exact same criteria as those we have used in the previous chapters: we need to consider output capability (spl) frequency response and dispersion. Since the monitor loudspeakers will be on stage with the performers and the audience came to see those performers and not to see the monitors, a low profile is important. Of course, the ultimate in 'low profile' monitors are the in-ear type where the monitor sound is fed directly to a pair of discrete earphones worn by the performer via a radio link. It is often necessary to create a reasonably high power sound field across the whole stage to give a feeling of the whole perfomance to those on stage, and the loudspeakers to do this are usually called side fills. And they can be larger since the audience don't really see them.

Objectives

The objective of stage monitoring is to support the performers. They need to hear each other in a certain way in order to be able to make their performance work. Each performer will need to hear different aspects of what the others are doing and fig. 10.1 shows an example of this.

This stage has been kept quite simple for illustration purposes but the principle is pretty typical. For example:

- The **drummer** likes quite a bit of his own kit to give the performance 'energy'. He needs the bass guitar as they work together as the foundations of the sound. Otherwise he takes some lead from the keyboards and a little vocals are needed for cues.
- The **bass guitar** has his own backline so he can hear that just fine and

doesn't need himself in his monitor. He's next to the drummer so he can hear that OK but he does need a little brass. He needs quite a bit of guitar, some keyboards and main vocal.

- The **brass** needs quite a bit of herself as she is rather close to the drummer and bass player's backline. Then she needs keyboards, guitar and vocals.
- **Keyboard**, like bass guitar has his own backline so doesn't need any of himself and is close enough to the guitar's backline to not need anything from that in the monitor. He needs main vocal and a little backing vocal, quite a bit of bass guitar and some brass.
- **Backing vocals** need quite a bit of themselves, and they get most pitch information from the keyboards so they need plenty of that. Main vocal and some brass complete their mix.
- **Main Vocal,** again needs a lot of herself, a good amount of keyboards and guitar and some backing vocals.
- **Guitar** has his own backline so he can hear himself easily. Bass guitar is a strong requirement with quite a bit of keyboard. Main vocal is needed for cues.

The important thing about creating monitor mixes is to work with the band and deliver what they need. As you build a rapport with a band

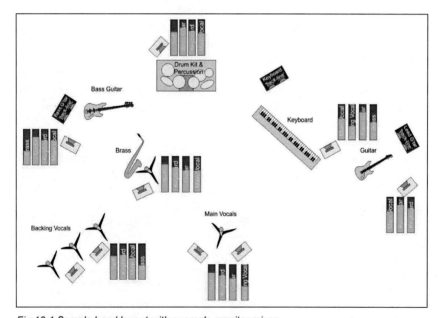

Fig 10.1 Sample band layout with example monitor mixes.

you'll get to know what they need and how they work. A monitor engineer often spends as much time on stage during a sound check as he/she will behind the mixing console. He/she will be talking to the band, listening to the mixes in situ and fine tuning their requirements.

Turn stuff down as well as up.

One very important point about stage monitor mixes is that of controlling the levels on stage; it is very easy to keep adding to mixes and let them creep up in level. When this process gets out of control you will make everything very difficult for everybody. Excessing monitor levels on stage mean:

- that the front of house sound basically become damage limitation of the excessive levels from stage.
- the feedback potential becomes much greater and the monitor engineer will spend most of his/her time controlling feedback rather than fine tuning mixes.
- the stage levels will become a health and safety concern not only for the band but all other crew in the area.

To help manage this, consider that a request for 'I need more <insert instrument here> in my monitor' could well be read as 'I need less of everything but <insert instrument here> in my monitor'.

Monitor Loudspeakers

One of the main differences between loudspeakers intended for stage monitor applications and those intended for 'main system' applications is the physical shape. Fig. 10.2 shows a typical wedge-monitor loudspeaker. The cabinet is cut so that when you lie it on the stage, it points directly at a person's head who is standing a short distance behind it. Often there are two faces cut at different angles to give a 'long-throw' or 'short-throw' option.

Like the loudspeakers we looked at for the main system a well behaved loudspeaker with even pattern control is essential in a stage monitor, in some ways even more so. If your loudspeaker has a unpredictable response then predicting and controlling feedback will be very difficult as the relationship between the monitors and microphones change as performers move around the stage.

Fig. 10.2 Typical 15" wedge-monitor loudspeaker.

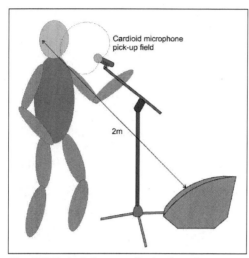

Fig. 10.3 Typical stage monitor loudspeaker arrangement.

(Within the image: "Cardioid microphone pick-up field", "2m")

This example has a 60°conical dispersion and an output of up to 136 dB spl. So we do need to be careful as this is easily capable of damaging hearing with even relatively short exposures. If we look at a typical arrangement as shown in fig. 10.3 we can see how this works. The microphone is actually slightly closer to the monitor than the performer so controlling feedback is a fine balancing act. Use of a directional (cardioid) microphone is essential (see chapter 14). The more directional the monitor speaker, the more focused the sound and so less is heard by adjacent performer and the less the sound becomes a cacophony.

Drum Fills

The drummer often needs quite a high monitor level to 'energise' his or her performance; in addition he/she needs a high level of other information to be able to hear it over the natural sound of the drum kit, assuming it is an acoustic kit. If it is an electronic kit the situation is somewhat different. Often a small PA stack or wedge monitor with a substantial sub-bass speaker is used as a drum-fill to deliver not only the level but also the extended low frequency range so that the drummer can 'feel' the sound.

Another option is a device which delivers low frequency energy directly into the seat of the drummer. It basically uses the motor assembly from a loudspeaker without the loudspeaker, instead clamps onto the drum stool and creates a physical vibration which mimics the 'feel' of the sound. Not all drummers like this, but some won't use anything else. Similar devices are now available for home cinemas and gaming to deliver an exciting acoustic experience without shaking the house down.

Side Fills

Often side-fills are used to give the band a 'feel' for the performance as a whole with their individual monitors used to focus on things they really need to hear to keep time and pitch. The side fills are usually a very similar mix to that in the main audience system and they usually use near-field (so wide angle) main system loudspeakers with modest subs.

In-Ear Personal Monitor Systems

One of the greatest innovations in stage monitoring in recent years is the In-Ear monitor system which is basically a radio microphone system (see chapter 14) in reverse. There are wired versions available for keyboard players and drummers who are less mobile on stage but the majority of them are wireless radio systems.

The basic principle of in-ear monitors is the same as for wedge-monitors in that each performer (or group of performers) can have his/her own personalised mix with only the instruments and performer that he/she needs to hear. The big difference is that with in-ear systems (often call IEMs for In Ear Monitors) only the person wearing them can hear them, and the sound level on stage is much more controlled instead of having many different mixes blaring out of lots of different speakers in a relatively small space. The other big advantage is that a performer can be much more mobile around the stage whilst maintaining the same mix which is impossible to achieve with conventional wedge monitors.

When using IEM systems, some 'ambient mics' are often fed into each mix. This provides a more realistic sound field and helps to break the sense of isolation that people often feel when using IEMs. It also means that if somebody were to shout a safety warning then everybody would hear it and not just those people without closely fitting IEM ear moulds.

Another 'trick' which can make the IEMs more of a realistic experience is to add a small amount of delay to their signal. If you look back at fig. 10.3 you'll see that the wedge monitor is about 2m from the performer's ears. This 2m is approximately 6ms (0.006 seconds). On the other hand the sound into the IEM ear-phone is practically instantaneous[1] which is a very unnatural situation. In an unamplified rehearsal room a performer might get 10ms or more before he/she hears himself reflected from a wall or other reflective surface. Consequently adding 6ms or more of electronic delay to the IEM mix can greatly enhance the experience for the performer. I often find myself in conversations about how this delay will affect a musician's ability to 'time' properly, to which my response is

---

1   Digital consoles and processing often add a few ms of 'latency' but not enough to make a
    real difference in this environment.

that even at 200 beats per minute (which is pretty fast) a single beat is 300ms (0.3 seconds). So this delay is 2% (two hundredths) of that beat time which is insignificant.

11

CONTROLLERS, CROSSOVERS AND AMPLIFIERS

Since these devices are such an integral part of the loudspeakers and thus the overall performance of your loudspeaker system, I felt that they deserved a short chapter of their own, separate from a discussion about using the loudspeakers themselves. As we have seen, the ideal situation of a single drive unit handling the wide entire range of frequency is just impossible to achieve, especially at the high powers necessary in public address systems. So we need to divide up the frequency spectrum into various 'bands' and then feed these into drivers suitable for that a range. How that is done is broadly classified into two groups which are called *passive* or *active*.

Passive Loudspeakers

Passive loudspeakers use a single channel of an amplifier and the process of splitting the frequency range into the bands for the various drivers is handled by an internal *crossover* circuit, sometimes called a crossover

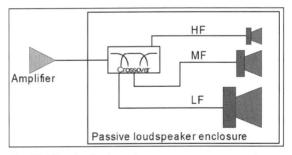

Fig. 11.1 Passive loudspeaker crossover arrangement.

network, see fig. 11.1. This system is cost effective as it reduces the number of expensive amplifiers needed for any given loudspeaker. Most small loudspeakers including practically all domestic loudspeakers fit into this category. The biggest problem with this design is that the frequency dividing process is done in the high current environment between the amplifier and the loudspeaker driver and this limits the processing that can be applied. Also, as power handling goes up, larger components are required which tend to be less efficient and the whole system starts to lose efficiency as heat.

Active Loudspeakers

Active loudspeakers move the complexities of frequency division into the low voltage low current signal level before the amplifier as shown in fig. 11.2. In this domain much more processing can be added and users can be given some control over the parameters where appropriate. The physical limitations of such things as driver alignment and resonance can be addressed by putting equalisation and delay into the signal path for a specific driver. The power output to the drivers can be monitored to some degree to help protect the drivers from damage through misuse. Overall the advantages of active system place them ahead of passive solutions in all areas except cost; active systems require an amplifier channel per frequency band which is both expensive and adds complexity and weight (of the amplifiers) to the system as a whole potentially reducing ease of transport.

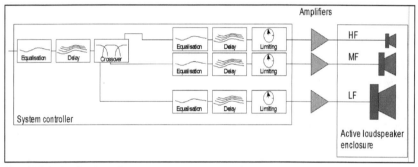

Fig. 11.2 Active loudspeaker crossover arrangement.

Hybrid Systems

Often hybrid systems between fully active and fully passive systems are employed. For example, in a three way system (high frequency, midrange

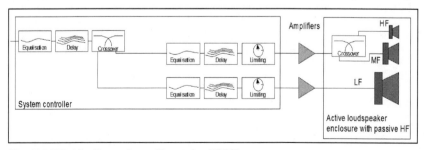

Fig. 11.3 Hybrid active system with passive HF/MF crossover.

and low frequency) the high-midrange and high frequency driver may be passively crossed-over and the low-midrange and low-frequency actively crossed-over as in fig. 11.3. This would reduce the amplifier requirements to two channels per cabinet instead of three and since the high frequency and high-midrange require substantially less power than the low frequency units, the associated problems are greatly reduced with an acceptable compromise yielding a reasonable cost saving.

Amplifier Controller Systems

The next option is to combine all the electronics into the same box so that the amplifier(s) and the system controllers are all combined into one unit. This can then be used with either completely active systems (with and amplifier channel per driver unit) or as a hybrid active/passive systems (where some drivers are fed from a crossover within the loudspeaker) as shown in fig. 11.4. Many amplifiers now carry a substantial amount of on board digital signal processing (DSP) and this allows for precise control over large loudspeakers systems without the need for racks of processing gear and all the associated wiring that is required to get it working. This also allows manufacturers to very precisely match the system control and management parameters to the loudspeakers' and amplifiers' characteristics and optimise the system performance and reliability.

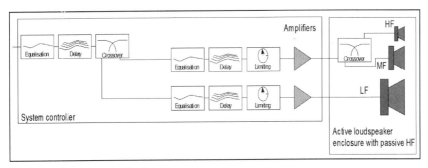

Fig. 11.4 Amplifier Controller System.

Powered Loudspeakers

The next option is to put all of this into the loudspeaker itself – which are usually called *powered loudspeakers*.

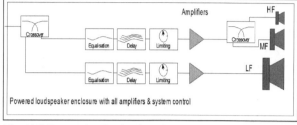

Fig. 11.5 Powered active loudspeaker.

Remote Control & Control Bus

By putting all this system processing either into the loudspeaker, into an amplifier or into a system processor (which is usually located with the amplifiers), you have simplified the system electronics but also introduced a problem: if you want to make the best of the powerful DSP available and that is located backstage in a rack room somewhere, or even up in the air inside your loudspeakers then your control interface for this system is not located by your control console where you need it. For this reason most manufacturers have developed software interfaces which allow you remotely control and monitor your system from a convenient location. Usually this software also allows you to build custom user interfaces so that you can group controls together in convenient ways.

How the computer and the amplifiers/system-controllers communicate differs between manufacturers but they are all based on some kind of control bus technology. Many use some kind of multi-drop serial bus network system such as RS485 (on which many others including DMX are based) or CAN bus. Some take these systems and give then their own brand name such as Tannoy's V-Net. The advantage of these types of systems is that they're well proven and inherently stable with cable runs up to (and some cases exceeding 1000m) so long as you follow the manufacturer's guidance to the letter. The scope of setting up such networks is beyond the scope of this book but I will just say that if the manufacturer says to use 110 Ohm cable (such as that specified for DMX or AES/EBU digital audio) then do so; this type of cable might look like normal microphone cable only more expensive but it is not and data integrity, which is the key to these systems performing well and reliably in the heat of the event, will be severely compromised by using the wrong type of cable.

Many systems are now capable of being controlled directly over

Ethernet. This has the advantage of configurability with the possibility of many more devices being linked than on a CAN bus or RS485 type system. The disadvantage is that an individual cable is limited to 100m although the use of switches and even fibre optic convertors can extend that to many kilometres. One possible barrier is that some IT networking knowledge is required to build a reliable system and details of this are beyond the scope of this book.

Setting Up Controllers

To my mind, by far the best systems fall into either the amplifier controller or powered loudspeaker category. This is because the amplifier and the loudspeaker have been designed and built to function as a single unit – which they must be considered to be. Amplifier design can and does differ greatly and even units with equivalent specifications can sound very different when driving identical loudspeakers. This is down to differences in the amplifier architecture. Having the whole system from the same manufacturer reduces many unknowns and variables and makes for a more consistent system, which is important in the commercial world of audio systems where systems are usually hired – sometimes from more than one hire company.

There is also the thorny issue of system protection: how many ways can you destroy a loudspeaker system? If we ignore methods for which we cannot provide protection such as dropping them out of the truck on the load in or leaving them out in the rain lying on their backs so all the drivers get soaked, then we can look at two basic ways that cause damage in general use:

    1. Over excursion
    2. Over temperature

1: *Over Excursion* is caused by brief transients pushing the driver too far mechanically. This means that the moving component of the driver is forced to move physically further than it can tolerate and the suspension (being the part that holds the moving component into place) gets damaged or fails altogether. This could be a kick drum beat destroying a sub-bass driver or a triangle hit destroying a high frequency driver. Either way it is damage done by short term events which causes metal high frequency drivers to shatter or the paper or fibre of mid and low frequency drivers to tear. Over driving loudspeakers in this way may not cause instant failure but it will weaken the mechanical components within the drivers which will then fail due to fatigue.

2: *Over temperature* is caused by longer term events than over excursion. Think of a 100W light bulb and how hot that gets; now consider that many bass drivers operate in the 1000W range or even more and think how much heat the coils generate. How much heat depends entirely on the type of signal being replayed. Take two examples of electronic dance music which features constant high energy bass will keep the power driving the coil to a near maximum for hours allowing it to heat with little opportunity to cool, while the other example is a live five piece band with a couple of guitars, a bass, keyboards and drums with one or more people singing. In this case the majority of the bass energy comes from the kick drum, bass guitar and maybe keyboards, this will typically be much more transient than the electronic music example; some songs might be quieter than others, and there will probably be period of dialogue with the audience where songs are introduced and there is no low frequency content at all. All of this gives the coils a chance to cool down and the average power fed to them will be considerably lower over the course of an evening.

The loudspeaker coils are just copper or aluminium wire coated with a thin varnish-type substance which forms an electrical insulation. When these coils get too hot the varnish starts to burn and blister and eventually it will flake off. This causes the insulation to break down and coils start to short out as adjacent parts of the windings make contact through the failing insulation. So this presents a physically shorter amount of wire to the output of the amplifier so the impedance falls so the power goes up and so more heat is generated and a cycle of inevitable destruction starts until the coil gets so hot that the wire itself melts away.

So the question is how do we protect a loudspeaker system from these two very different types of damage: one caused by short duration high energy pulses leading to mechanical failure and the other long term excessive power which leads to thermal-electrical failure. An average power limiter will not react fast enough prevent the transient damage, whilst a peak limiter will not prevent the long term thermal damage.

With active systems it is possible to set limiters for each frequency band driver whereas with passive system you can only apply a global limiter setting for the entire set of components which can never be as accurate a method of protection. In the case of active controller systems and powered loudspeakers the parameters are set up and locked out by the manufacturer and they can be very precisely based on extensive testing so these do tend to be able to offer higher output systems when compared to more conventional controller based and purely passive systems. Some systems simply provide the controller parameter settings in tabular form that can be put into third party controllers of your choice. Here again is a problem because the amplifiers come after the controllers in the signal chain, and you need to know how those amplifiers will perform to be able to set any system protection with any degree of accuracy.

Finding the limit point value

Because dB are so easy to use we simply need to work out the maximum voltage that we can safely feed into the loudspeaker, convert this to dBu then subtract the amplifier voltage from this figure to get the limit point in dBu. This figure can be entered into your system processor and your limiter is set.

Maximum safe loudspeaker voltage

Most loudspeakers quote a maximum RMS power rating and nominal impedance. This can be converted into voltage using (see chapter 4).

$$v = \sqrt{PR}$$

where:
V is the voltage you are looking for, P is the RMS power rating and R is the nominal impedance.

For example an 8Ω loudspeaker with an RMS power rating of 850W has a maximum voltage input of √(850x8)=82.5V.

This needs to be converted to dBu (referenced to 0.775V) using:

$$dBu = 20 \log \frac{v}{0.775}$$

So in our example this is

$$dBu - 20 \log \frac{82.5}{0.775} - 40.5 dBu$$

If we have an amplifier with a voltage gain of 30dB then the limit point needs to be:

40.5 – 30 = +10.5 dBu

The '+' before the 10 isn't necessary but it avoids confusion.

So we can combine this into one limit point formula:

$$Limit\ Point\ in\ dBu = 20 \log \frac{\sqrt{PR}}{0.775} - AmpGain\ in\ dB$$

where P is the RMS power rating of the loudspeaker in Watts, R is the loudspeaker nominal impedance in Ohms and the amplifier voltage gain in dB.

If this all seems a bit much there's a spread sheet to do it for you at www.rolandhigham.co.uk/spreadsheets.

Maximum amplifier gain

It is very important that the amplifier gain is set in such a way that it cannot be set any higher than the value you used to calculate the limit point. If it isn't, then there is nothing to stop somebody from just turning the amplifier up and so adding more gain after the limiter and thus sending too much power into the loudspeaker.

If there are gain range switches (usually hidden on the rear panel of the amplifier somewhere) these should always be set as low as possible. There are two reasons for this:

It keeps the overall system noise as low as possible.

It keeps digital system processors running as close to their optimum resolution as possible.

Maximum amplifier power

So far we have assumed here that the world is perfect and that there is no such thing as maximum amplifier power. Since that isn't the case we need to ensure that we aren't expecting the amplifier to deliver more power than it is capable of and thus drive it into clip. The easiest way to do this is to specify amplifiers which are at least 25% over the maximum loudspeaker power; 25% only gives you about 1dB headroom, so if your budget can stretch that far you should aim to be 50% or more over for greatest headroom and performance. The other alternative is to reduce the limit point to stop the amplifier clipping, although this could start to have a detrimental effect on your sound quality.

The simplest way to check the limit point is to put the amplifier output power and the impedance this is quoted for, into the formula above, ignoring G (voltage gain) and see check that this value is over the limit point for the speaker system. If it isn't, either change your amplifier or use this value (usually at least -1db) instead.

12 USING MICROPHONES

Loudspeakers take electrical signals and turn them into acoustic sound energy: microphones do the exact opposite by taking acoustic sound energy and turning that into electrical signals. We have looks at how to consider best usage and placement of loudspeakers in some detail and now we will look at the equally important technique of using microphones. With the loudspeakers and the microphones in the correct places, then you are most of the way to completing the job successfully. If 45% of the job is getting the right loudspeakers in the right place, then another 45% is getting the right microphones in the right place. The remaining 10% is twiddling the knobs to add the 'gloss'. These 'figures' are by no means carefully researched statistics but they do illustrate the importance of getting the physical things right first. However, one of the advantages of microphones is that we can usually 'play' with their position far more easily and readily during the setup and rehearsal process than we can with loudspeakers. And indeed it is usually good practice to do so, in fact if you don't like the sound of an instrument or voice, before you do anything to the controls on you console, examine the position of the microphone.

Before we even consider which type of microphone is best for an application let us look at the natural sound sources that we are likely to encounter. Here are some common and less common examples that I have encountered:

- Human voice
- Trumpet
- Violin
- Guitar
- Snare drum
- Saw
- Squeaky rubber chicken
- Motorcycle sprocket hit with a wooden hammer
- A pit of broken glass

For those with a mind for study and research, much has been published on the directivity and characteristics of most common instruments dating back over many years and the work of (for example) Jurgen Meyer is well worth reading. That said much can be learnt from a little practical experimentation and, when presented with some of the more random and obscure items that you're likely to meet then experimentation is the only way of proceeding.

One such method is simply to place your ear where you think you might want to place the microphone. Obviously take care as to your personal safety both from a point of view of noise exposure and personal injury. If you can't safely get your own ear in right place, then try positioning a microphone whilst monitoring the direct sound from it into a pair of good headphones. This is usually easier with two people – one to listen and one to position the microphone. Once you have found a position that you like, double check that it doesn't impede the musician (or anybody else on the stage). For example a mic placed low down in front of a cello can be easily knocked by a vigorous bow and a mic stand that starts the show too close to a drummer may well finish it several metres away on its side picking the sound of a smoke machine!

Often you will be expected to 'mic' an already amplified source – for example, an electric guitar or other electronic instrument. In such cases there may be a suitable 'line output' available to connect the instrument or its local amplifier directly to your system, or a DI box can be used in the same way, but it is not uncommon for the loudspeaker cabinet itself to contribute to the characteristic sound that the musician wants to create and, in this case, we must take the sound from the output of that loudspeaker – which is to put a microphone in front of it. Here you can find great differences between the tone from the centre of the loudspeaker to the edge, or from a mic at an inch or less to one placed a foot away. Always talk to the musician where ever possible and see if he/she has any preferences. Such preferences may be based on hours of tinkering around in a studio with less time pressure than a live event and save you time. Some microphones are specifically designed to be used on 'backline' loudspeakers in this way such as the Sennheiser E-609, but often a musician may have his or her own personal preference and may even carry their preferred mic with them.

Basic Types of Microphone

Microphones come in three basic types:

- **Omnidirectional** – which pick up sound equally from all directions.
- **Unidirectional** – which attenuate (or reject) sounds coming from certain direction(s).
- **Others** – this may seem a little vague, but this category excludes the two

common types listed above and includes contact mics and boundary layer mics.

All simple, small microphones are omnidirectional – that is they pick up sounds evenly from all directions. Actually the limitation to this is (just like loudspeakers) that they become more directional as the wavelength approaches the size of the capsule; in the case of microphones this 'directionality' starts when the capsule diameter is $1/_{10}$ of the wavelength being considered. So for a capsule with a diameter of 1cm (0.01m) it will start to become directional above about 3.4kHz. For this reason precision test microphones for use with highly accurate audio analysis systems have very small capsules on long tubular mountings. To have a truly omnidirectional microphone up to 20kHz would require a capsule of slightly less about $1^3/_4$mm in diameter – which is something of a manufacturing challenge and carries a high price tag.

If you can compare the behaviour of the smaller (and so more expensive) head-worn type of microphone capsules (favoured by theatre shows) and some of the larger, cheaper ones supplied with budget radio mic systems, apart from the fact that the more expensive 'heads' sound much better anyway – listen to the difference when you speak into the front of the capsule as against if you speak into the side or rear (by the cable entry point). You will usually find that the cheaper devices with comparatively large capsules sound progressively 'duller' (that is they lose their ability to reproduce high frequency) as you move around the back of them.

The great thing about omnidirectional mics is that they have no complications: they are a single transducer open to the air at the front and sealed at the back; compare this with cardioid mics that we look at in the next few paragraphs. It is the simplicity of the omnidirectional microphone that usually makes them very natural sounding and if you're working in a good 'environment' like a well-designed concert hall or recording studio then they 'hear' that environment too which can be very advantageous. Unlike unidirectional mics they don't suffer from the *proximity effect*; it is far easier to get a flat frequency response from them. So if you're recording then omnidirectional mics are often favoured, but this isn't a book about recording – it is a book about live sound and the problems for the live sound designer and engineers include *gain before feedback* and *channel separation* – both of which are significantly compromised by the use of omnidirectional microphones. So with the exception of very close mics such as head-worn radio mic systems for singers and some instrument-mounted equivalents, omnidirectional microphones are very rare on the live sound stage.

By contrast to the simplicity of omni directional mics, unidirectional mics use some method to exclude sound from behind the capsule and to some extent the sides. The most common technique is to allow the sound that arrives at the rear of the capsule to pass through holes or slots and tubes so that an acoustic delay within the capsule housing is created. This is then arranged so that sound arriving directly from the front of the microphone is largely unaffected but as the source moves to the side then a phase shift starts to occur which progressively cancels out sounds from increasing angles off the centre axis. One side effect of this technique is the *proximity effect*.

Proximity Effect

As long as your source is some considerable distance away from your microphone capsule then these path-length/phase shift techniques to control directivity work well, but as the microphone gets closer to the source, then the path-length difference between the 'front' and the 'rear' of the capsule becomes significant (by application of the inverse square law) but at longer wavelengths the phase shift is minimal, so you get an increase is the low frequency sensitivity of the microphone as the source is brought closer to that microphone. The exact 'shape' of the increase (its tonality and level) is dependent on the microphone design but typically you can expect a rise of around 10dB below 100Hz. For some situations the rise could be as high as 16dB. Now this may not be a bad thing and some microphones may sound better as a result – the Shure SM58, for example is often used with a vocalist practically touching the metal gauze with his/her lips. This close proximity gives a natural boost to the vocal sound, adding warmth and fullness without the need to add electronic boost which would cause feedback. The low frequency boost at close range is called the *proximity effect*.

Many experienced performers will use this boost to their benefit. For example many trumpet and trombone players have learnt that backing away from the mic gives them a different tone than being up close. A good monitor engineer will arrange for the performers monitors to reflect this and allow the performer to maximise their control over their environment. Even stand-up comedians use this and often create various comic vocal effects by microphone positioning.

Microphones and loudspeakers can be thought of in very similar terms – they both transform energy between electrical and acoustic forms: loudspeakers make acoustic energy out of electrical energy and microphones make electrical out of acoustic energy. You can use a small loudspeaker (such as that in a pair of headphones) as a microphone and you can use a dynamic mic (such as an SM58) as a small loudspeaker. In fact the SM58 signal monitor is an oft-used emergency fault finding technique – have a look at chapter 17, Simple Fault Finding. So it should come as no surprise to learn that microphones come with (or should do) charts detailing their directivity that are very similar to those produced for loudspeakers: polar plots, Isobar graphs, etc.

However, since microphones do not have to handle large amounts of electrical power (and the heat that goes with that) their design is usually much less compromised than that of a loudspeaker, and so their directional behaviour and frequency response is usually much more ideal. For example, most microphones are a round tube with a capsule at one end and (unlike a loudspeaker) as long as you point the 'tube' in the right direction, it doesn't matter how the tube is rotated. That is the microphone does not have a different shape of pick-up field in the plane of the manufacturer's badge than it does at right angles to it! This means that the pick-up pattern diagrams for microphones are usually much less complex than those for loudspeakers. See fig. 12.1. You will see from fig. 12.1 that, like loudspeakers, microphones do have different responses at different frequencies but there tends to be much less variance.

Cardioid is a term derived from mathematics for a (roughly) circular shape with a bit taken out of it. The 500 Hz curve in fig 12.1 is the best example of this shape. Another 'shape' of polar pattern you will meet is the hypercardioid as shown in fig. 12.2. You might also meet supercardioid but to all intents and purposes this is as close enough to hypercardioid as makes no difference.

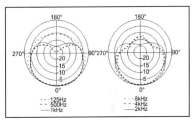

Fig 12.1 Typical polar pattern for a cardioid microphone.

For situations where you need to pick sounds quite a long way away there are *shotgun* microphones which have a very elongated chamber behind the capsule such as that shown in fig. 12.3 with a polar plot shown in fig. 12.4.

At this point it is worth mentioning the side-pick-up type of microphone which are usually large diaphragm condenser types or dynamic mics for special purposes such as drum mics. In these the

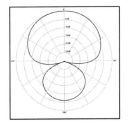

Fig. 12.2 Ideal hypercardioid polar pattern.

capsule is arranged at right angles to the mounting tube. The key to using these is that

Fig 12.3 AKG C568 shotgun microphone.

the manufacturer's logo usually indicated the centre of the capsule and this should face the instrument of sound source as shown in fig. 12.5.

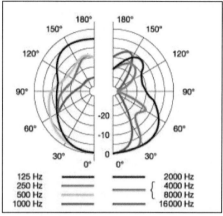

125 Hz	2000 Hz
250 Hz	4000 Hz
500 Hz	8000 Hz
1000 Hz	16000 Hz

Fig. 12.4 AKG C568 polar plot.

Fig. 12.5 AKG C3000 with capsule and pick-up field overlaid.

Another example is the classic kick-drum mic shown in fig. 12.6. This again has the capsule set at right angles to the mounting tube.

Other Types of Microphone

Our third category of microphones type covers all other designs which include boundary microphones or pressure zone microphones (PZM) such as fig. 12.7.

These mics are designed to be mounted onto a hard surface and

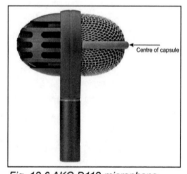
Fig. 12.6 AKG D112 microphone showing capsule position.

effectively turn that surface into one large microphone element with a hemispherical (half a sphere) pick-up pattern. This is done by placing a small capsule as close to the surface as is practical and in so doing they ensure that both the direct and reflected sound are in phase as shown in fig. 12.7.

Such microphones are of limited use on the live stage as they need to be fixed to a reasonable large surface to offer a wide frequency range and their hemispherical pattern can limit gain before feedback if they are placed so that you can actually see the performer around them! That

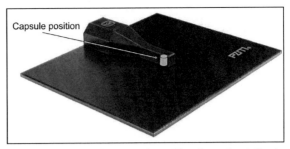

Fig. 12.7 PZM showing capsule position drawn in relation to the plate.

said thre are a few applications where they can perform well. One such application is inside the lid of grand pianos where you already have a reasonably large flat hard surface in the form of the lid. The same applies to a lesser degree in upright pianos.

Some boundary microphones mount through the boundary itself. Again these are of limited use on the live stage but occasionally an application will present itself. An example of this is shown in fig. 12.8

Fig. 12.8 'Through-plate' boundary mic.

There are also some specialist contact mics such as those made by C-ducer for all kinds of applications from pianos to banjos. These are a microphone 'strip' which gets stuck with tape to the instrument in question. The section of the instrument to which the C-ducer tape is attached then behaves similar to the plate in a boundary-type microphone.

How Microphones Work

The method by which the acoustic energy is converted into electrical energy comes in two types:

Dynamic – which is basically a loudspeaker in reverse in that the sound directly affects a diaphragm onto which is fixed a coil of wire that moves through a magnetic field and generates a voltage which produces the output. This type of microphone is pretty self-contained and does not require *phantom power* unlike the condenser types detailed next. So they can be used in situations where phantom power is not available, such as talk-back systems and simple budget PA applications. Dynamic microphones tend to be very robust but tend to have lower sensitivity.

Condenser – in which the sound energy affects a diaphragm suspended in an electric field. This also includes *electret* mics where the electric field is permanently *etched* into the capsule using clever chemistry similar to that used to make semiconductors. This technique is now the most common type of microphone as pretty much every mobile phone, PC and other consumer device with a microphone in it, uses the electret type as they as are cheap to make and very reliable. Manufacturing technology means that these can now also be made to a very high standard and they are increasingly found in the 'pro market'.

In the case of non-electret condensers electrical power is required to make the electric field, fig. 12.10. In the case of electret mics, power is needed to amplify the minute output from the fixed field to a useful level fig. 12.9, so all condenser microphones (electret or otherwise) require a power supply of sorts. In some cases this is simply a battery which is ideal for portable equipment such as camera mounted microphones for TV shoots and news gathering, but less ideal for a live stage because a battery failure is not acceptable. For our purposes on the live stage *phantom power* is used whereby (usually) the mixing console provides a 48 volt supply. On smaller and budget consoles this may be a single switch that applies power to all channels or on larger and more sophisticated ones it will be on individual channels, although there might also a master switch hidden away somewhere.

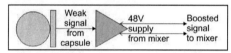

Fig. 12.9 Electret microphone phantom power application.

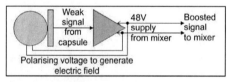

Fig. 12.10 Condenser microphone phantom power application.

Beware of phantom power under normal circumstances. With well-designed and robust professional equipment, phantom power is either required or simply ignored. But with some devices – especially those with unbalanced outputs (typically electronic instruments or domestic and computer equipment such as MP3 players and laptops) applying phantom power will usually result in a combination of the following: acrid smell, wisps of smoke and failure of the device in question. Such devices should only be connected to console line inputs that cannot have phantom power on them (check the manual for confirmation of this) or if such inputs are unavailable or if there is any doubt then the device should be connected via an isolating transformer or DI box.

DI Boxes

A DI or Direct Injection Box allows an unbalanced device such as an electric guitar, keyboard or computer with a high impedance unbalanced output to drive a low impedance balanced input of the type found on mixing console inputs. In so doing to protects the device from accidentally receiving phantom power – which is usually fatal to the device!

Fig. 12.11 EMO Passive Direct Injection (DI) box.

Basic DI boxes are simply an isolating transformer with jack or RCA/ phono inputs and XLR output, fig. 12.11.

These usually have various input ranges such as low-level instrument for electric guitars, line input for keyboards MP3 players, or other similar 'pre-amplified' devices and high level inputs that can accept the output of the backline amplifier at speaker level. The input type is usually determined by which input socket you use. These have two sockets for loudspeaker and instrument inputs so that the DI box can be put in between the instrument and its amplifier if necessary.

Fig. 12.12 BSS Active DI box.

This type of DI box is cost effective and extremely robust. It needs no phantom power and I have seen somebody literally drive a car over one at an outdoor event (accidentally); it suffered no damage apart from needing a bit of a clean!

Beyond this there are increasing levels of cost and complexity such as that shown in fig. 12.12. which has become a de facto standard. It has jack or XLR input and link out on ¼" jack sockets and a balanced input on XLR. The input signal range is selected by a simple toggle switch for instrument (0dB), line (-20dB) and loudspeaker level (-40dB). The dB figures refer to the amount of *padding* or attenuation that is applied to the input signal to reduce its level. Although it runs off phantom power there is a 9V battery option for the occasions when 48V phantom power is not available. Despite these added features, the essential function is always the same as the passive device shown in fig. 12.11. And a sample application is shown in fig. 12.13.

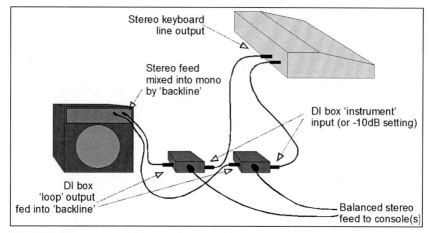

Fig 12.13 Common use of DI boxes for electronic instruments.

Choosing the best microphone for the job

The choice of microphone is probably even more subjective for a given application than the choice of any other device in the signal chain. To this end many, many hours of informed discussions have taken place on stages, in recording studios, in tour buses and especially in pubs and bars as to the *best* microphone to use on a particular instrument (or voice) for a particular performer. The subtle nuances that separate microphones are way beyond the scope of any written text and ultimately only trial and error will find that perfect microphone for John's nose flute solo (or whatever the subject of the discussion is). That said you can eliminate a great deal of the trial and error by eliminating some things that just won't work. For example, dynamic microphones tend to be less sensitive than condenser types – that is you need more sound pressure impinging onto the microphone to generate the same voltage output, so using dynamic mics on very quiet sources can bring your noise floor up to unacceptably high levels. Another example is the Sennhesier MKH 40 – which has to be one of my favourite microphones of all time, being very well engineered, versatile and sounds fantastic on pretty much anything, *except* that it is very sensitive to wind noise. Consequently I have found that this makes it unsuitable for use on outdoor stages unless they are *very well* sheltered and I have to settle for cheaper alternatives to deliver the goods unless extensive wind shielding is brought in and that takes time and can look unsightly. As with many engineering solutions it may well be that the best theoretical solution just doesn't work in the cold bath of reality!

If you are working with a particular group of musicians for an extended period of time, then you can experiment with the best microphones and the best ways to use them. Take note of what devices and techniques they might have used in the studio, but be aware of the very different challenges presented by the live stage environment (such as wind noise).

Generally speaking condenser mics will perform better in the vast majority of applications. But on average they cost between twice or even ten times more than a perfectly good dynamic mic, and expensive ones are vastly more expensive. So in most situations you will need to find a cost-based compromise of the best mics available for the job – usually from what is in you stock or the hire company supplying the gear. So with this in mind, dynamic mics are good for:

- Hand-held vocals as they are robust and do not suffer from handling noise. Also they are much less susceptible to 'breath pops' than condensers.
- Brass and loud woodwind as these are loud instruments and the dynamic mic handles them well. In addition the lack of susceptibility to wind and breath noise makes them ideal when close mic'ing such instruments.
- Close mic'ing drums and percussion as there are a number of specialist types which literally clip directly onto the drum itself; their robustness here a key factor in this application.

Condenser mics are good for:

- More distant applications such as percussion over-heads, or group mic'ing such as two mics for a small string section.
- Detailed spoken word – such as conference presentation. In these applications the presenter is usually more comfortable when they are at some distance (i.e. more than a couple of inches from the microphone).

Microphone positioning

Choosing the best microphone position is, like most other things we have discussed, a matter of finding the best compromise. Close mic positions are good for gain-before-feedback (as we saw in chapter 9) and the proximity effect might be useful, however, close mic positions are usually tonally coloured in that they inevitably favour one part of the instrument over another and the true 'sound' of that instrument is a combination of all the sounds it radiates. For example, look at the options presented in fig. 12.14.

Fig. 12.14 possible mic possible positions for an acoustic guitar.

A. Close position with high string bias. This position will favour the high strings and due to the hand position you will probably get a reasonable bias of the sound hole which gives you a lot of mid-range.

B. Close position close to the bridge. This will give you the 'harder' sound from the bridge with no particular string bias.

C. Close position close to low strings. This will give you a low string bias with the hand shielding the sound hole.

D. Distance position. This will give you the most neutral sound but at the expense of gain before feedback.

There are many options for direct attachments of microphones to instruments, and most of these will arrive with the musicians. As always talk to the musicians and see what they usually do.

Radio Microphones

So far we have looked at microphones which connect directly to the mixing console with a cable, however performers often do not want to be tethered by a cable when they are on a stage and the solution is the *radio microphone*. A radio microphone (as its name suggests) uses a radio transmitter in (or connected to) the microphone to send the signal to a radio receiver which is then connected to the mixer as a wired microphone would be. Radio microphones come in three basic types:

Hand-held, where the transmitter is built into the body of the microphone and is held in the performer's hand as a normal cabled microphone would be. Or it could be mounted on a microphone stand (but much more mobile without the cable). These microphones are not much bigger than a standard wired microphone and come in many types with plenty of capsule options.

Lavalier, or tie-clip type. These can either (as the name suggests) be clipped onto the performer's clothing although far better results are usually achieved by hiding them on the performer's head or hair or even (more blatantly) in the form a direct headset where a head-worn frame holds the microphone directly in front of the performer's mouth.

Transmitter only systems – these are either designed to take an instrument input from (for example) an electric guitar or other portable instrument or a microphone input from a dynamic microphone.

The acoustic principles of using radio microphones don't differ from those of wired microphones; in the case of head-worn microphones, you can get the microphone much closer to the performer's mouth and so (applying the inverse-square law) you get much more *level* into the microphone and so your gain before feedback is about as high as you can possibly achieve.

Radio microphones use radio transmission and so they need some space in the radio spectrum to operate. This typically fits into three categories:

VHF – uses the frequency range 173MHz to 175MHz and 191MHz to 209MHz.

These frequencies generally fit around various radio transmissions such as FM radio and DAB.

UHF – uses the frequency range 470Mhz to 865MHz.

These fit amongst digital terrestrial TV and the usage is being squeezed by demand for more channels for mobile data coverage.

WiFi & DECT Bands - uses 1.9GHz (DECT) and 2.4GHz to 2.5GHz (WiFi).

Note that these frequencies are those for the UK, other countries may have different restrictions and availability so always check local information. In addition to frequency restrictions, the power output of the transmitter is carefully controlled and typically these are 10mW for hand-held type and 50mW for body-worn units. The higher power for the latter allows for energy absorbed by the human body. The *width* (i.e. how many kHz or mHz of spectrum it takes up) of each channel is down to the design, and the manufacturer's manual should have details of which channels can be used together without interference. Each microphone you intend to use will take up one channel – you cannot transmit with more than one transmitter on any one channel and if you try you will hear a characteristic whistle caused by interference between the two carrier frequencies.

In order to use these channels the frequency management is handled (in the UK) by Arqiva and information relating to the use of radio microphones should be sought from them. The following information is correct at the time of writing but may change without notice, so always check the licensing authority information and be aware that even the licensing organisation has changed several times over the last few years too!

Generally the 170MHz VHF channels are licence free as is the upper end of the UHF spectrum (863MHz to 865MHz) but as a consequence these can be quite congested especially in towns and cities. Although the range of such radio microphone systems is quite short and the radio signal is heavily attenuated by building structures, many pubs and clubs have radio microphone systems as do universities and corporate meeting rooms so if you rely on these frequencies you may have a problem.

On the other hand Arqiva (currently) can give you (at a cost) specific frequencies that are available in the upper VHF band and lower UFH band but these are likely to only be available in certain parts of the country in the 'gaps' between TV channels which vary from region to region.

The licence-free wifi range is very highly congested especially in built-up areas where there can often be many wifi access points all transmitting together. That said the DECT solution is popular in corporate environments as these systems are usually heavily encrypted so that sensitive information that may be discussed in meetings cannot be eavesdropped with a simple receiver unit – as is the case with conventional radio microphone systems. The audio quality and intelligibility of these systems is usually very good for the spoken word but not designed for musical use.

If you are using *radio in ear monitor* systems, don't forget that each of these systems uses a channel too and these must be built into your frequency plan with each transmitter taking up one channel. Don't forget however, that you can run as many receivers as you want for each channel you transmit. While this is rarely useful with microphones, it can simplify your event with monitors as groups of performers can share the same monitor *mix* in this way.

There are some digital radio microphone systems which like digital mobile phones and digital television systems use data compression to squeeze more 'channels' into the same band width with some cost in terms of both money and audio delay, though the audio delays are quite low in the order of 3ms or so. At the time of writing these haven't made much market progress in the live field but they are worth watching. As the RF spectrum available to us gets squeezed every tighter by the *big money* of mobile telecom data, solutions such as digital radio microphones have to become viable.

13 MIXERS

The mixer is your flight deck, it gives you all the control you need once your system is configured. If you have your loudspeakers in the right place and correctly configured and your microphones are correctly positioned, then you are most of the way there. That said there is always the capacity to get it horribly wrong in the mix. A careful and sensitive approach to mixing a show is essential and understanding how your mixer works is part of that process.

So, having looked at the tricky bits of getting sound into the electronic domain (using microphones, etc) and then getting the electronic signal back into sound (using loudspeakers), we need to look at how we combine, manipulate then distribute these electronic signals in a control environment and the central component in this process is the mixer or mixing console. Like most other pieces of equipment we encounter the mixer can be anything from a compact and easily portable device that is about the size of this book, all the way up to enormous thing that gives a grand piano a run for its money both in terms of weight and floor space.

Whether your mixer is an epensive and complex digital device or a budget compact analogue unit, the basic principle is the same. A mixer combines a number of input 'channels' which may be fed from microphones or direct from instruments or replay devices; there could also be feeds from other mixers such as broadcast mixes, satellite down-links or streamed over the internet; in fact they could be pretty much any audio source as long as they're less than around +16dBu. These input 'channels' are then combined into one (or more) 'busses' which then feed one (or more) outputs. Fig. 13.1 shows the basic principle.

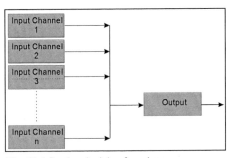

Fig. 13.1 Basic principle of a mixer.

Fig 13.2 shows a very simple example of a mixer which has a gain and single level control for six mic inputs with a stereo output with a single auxiliary output. There is some simple equalisation and two line inputs.

For anything but the simplest of task, a mixer will require

Fig. 13.2 Simple rack mounted mixer.

more features than this although the basic functionality remains the same. On any reasonable 'live' mixing console we would expect to see something like fig. 13.3 as a 'channel strip'. A 16 channel console would have 16 such channel strips and a 40 channel would have 40 of them.

Over the past few years we have seen a renaissance in console design as large format digital consoles are becoming cheaper to produce and better featured than large format analogue consoles. In the past analogue consoles had always held the ace on sonic quality and useability but as technology advances and costs reduce, the days of the large format analogue console are numbered. Digital audio technology is now able to deliver the audio quality that engineers desire and the designers have worked hard integrating new technology into user interfaces that present all the controls quickly and efficiently to the engineer without having to scroll through confusing pages of options. Coupled with this are the virtually lossless digital transport systems that can move large number of channels through a single data cable or fibre optic link which replaces analogue multicores that are both bulky and heavy and contribute to signal losses over even relatively short distances of a few tens of metres.

The important thing to remember is that no matter how complex the console and how many features it offers, the basic premise is to combine all of the necessary input channels and mix then all together (providing the appropriate control) and then route them to the desired outputs. For example, if we have a small group of performers (say ten channels of microphone/DI box) on a simple stage with a stereo speaker system then a simple ten input into two output (written 10:2) mixer will suffice. Obviously if you only have a 16:2 to hand then you can use that one, whereas an 8:2 wouldn't fit as you don't have enough input channels.

In most case you would need a simple effects processor (maybe a reverb unit) to add a little 'life' which would add a couple of channels, although many small analogue consoles and most large format digital consoles have these built in.

FOH or Monitor Mixer

Let me illustrate this by considering two very different engineering roles that often co-exist at the same event on the same stage: Front of House (FOH) and Monitors.

The FOH engineer is charged with getting the sound balance right for the entire audience whether that audience numbers less than a hundred or tens of thousands. In most cases this involves taking all the input channels and making a stereo mix to fit the venue. Often the picture is made more complex with different groups of loudspeakers for different areas of the audience such as main PA, front fills and delays, etc. but for now let us just consider the main stereo PA system.

On the other hand the Monitor engineer has the job of making sure that each performer on the stage can hear what they need of the other performers in order to perform. In chapter 10 we looked at a conventional band scenario with a vocalist, some backing vocals, a guitarist or two, keyboards, bass guitar and a drummer and maybe a saxophone: the drummer often needs to hear the bass player, the keyboards and rhythm guitar, but doesn't need (or want) to hear the saxophonist or the backing singers. He probably needs the lead vocals to give a 'feel' of the event or to take specific cues from but they aren't as important to him all the time as the bassist. Conversely the lead vocalist might take all his pitch and timing from the keyboards and since the drummer is making enough noise on his own, he doesn't need (or want) drums in his monitor mix.

In a way the monitor engineer's job is the opposite of the FOH engineer's job in that they make many 'mixes' of a few channels instead of a few mixes of all of the channels.

For this reason the design of analogue mixing consoles differs greatly between FOH and Monitor roles: some monitor consoles don't even have faders on each channel, but they do have 20 or more 'auxiliary' sends per channel so that 20 or more different separate mixes could be created. Now, with flexible platform digital consoles and clever user interface design the same physical console can simply be set up as FOH or Monitor as desired.

Of course the harsh reality of the real world dictates that between these two extremes is the often difficult realm of one console operated by one engineer who has to fulfil both roles simultaneously. And this might be a small concert stage, a musical theatre show or any other type of event requiring sound reinforcement. And in such cases a general purpose analogue or digital console can be used to cover both bases with the channel faders being used for the FOH mix and pre-fade auxiliary send being used to generate a few monitor mixes as required. Here again the more configurable digital consoles can offer greater flexibility and controllability which ultimately leads to a better event.

Basic Channel Model

The channel strip shown in fig. 13.3 is very common on most small-medium format consoles and the principle applies as much to digital consoles as it does to analogue consoles. As we move up to more complex consoles we also get VCA-group assignment (often called DCAs on digital consoles), mute group or programme mute assignment, the auxiliaries have pre- or post-fade on each send and some (especially digital consoles) offer features such as dynamic processors (gates and compressors) and delay. The equalisation (eq) becomes more comprehensive, offering variable high and low frequency adjustment as well as Q (which varies the amount of the spectrum that you affect as you turn the frequency-gain knob).

Whether the console is analogue or digital, front of house or monitors, the basic signal path through the channel is the same, as we have seen above. Here I have listed the electronic elements in the order the signal passes through them. This is slightly different from the apparent signal path of the channel strip shown here which, although approximately the same order, is conventionally arranged for operational convenience.

Taking each section of this 'channel strip' in turn:

1a - First there's a gain knob
1b - with a high pass filter and 'phase' switch

1c - Then the '+48' phantom power switch and LED

2a - 4 band 'eq' with fixed HF and LF and two variable frequency mid bands.

2b - There's also an eq bypass switch

3a - Then we have six auxiliary sends which are switchable in pairs to be pre or post fade. Pre fade mixes remain at the same level regardless of the channel fader position and post fade mixes will vary in sympathy with the channel fader.
3b - Pre/Post send switch

4 - A *pan* control allows each mono channel to be placed anywhere in the stereo sound field.
5 - A channel mute switch mutes all sends whether pre or post fade from this channel.

6 - Routing switches send the channel (post pan control) to the stereo bus, groups 1 & 2, groups 3 & 4, groups 5 & 6 and groups 7 & 8.

7 - Channel fader with simple signal LEDs above it.

8 - Finally a pfl button allows the signal to be monitored (usually in headphones) pre fader but post EQ.

13.3 Example of a console 'channel strip'.

1. The first stage is the pre-amp which takes the signal as it arrives from the source (e.g. microphone). This has the gain control (a) which is used to set the initial level of the signal as it starts its journey through the mixing console. Typically it will be used to bring all levels up to around 0dB on the meter. There is a

high pass filter (b) although some consoles place this switch in the eq section. This switch sharply reduces signals below about 80Hz (the frequency varies with console design and may even be variable). This helps to reduce mic handling noise or other unwanted mechanical noise and proximity effects. This section also contains the 48V Phantom Power switch to power microphones and DI boxes (see chapter 12) and the Ø 'Phase' switch (c) which inverts the polarity of the waveform.

2. After the pre-amp stage, comes the equalisation section (2), where changes are made to the frequency response. The complexity of the eq varies with console design and some allow you to select a frequency and bandwidth and then apply cut or boost as required. This example just has a frequency selection knob with bandwidth fixed. There's also an EQ bypass switch (2b) to allow comparison between the adjusted signal and the raw one.

3. The next set of controls are the auxiliary sends (3a) which are grouped in pairs. Two of these pairs can be switched (3b) to be pre-fade or post-fade whilst the last pair are fixed post fade. On larger consoles these are usually selectable individually. Auxiliary sends allow 'mixes' to be generated from the channels; pre-fade mixes are independent of the fader position, as the name implies, and these are used for monitor mixes. On a console that is doing both FOH & monitors the FOH is controlled by the faders but the monitor mix remains independent. Post fade auxes are used for sends to effects processors or recorders.

4. The Pan knob, literally pans this channel between the left and right stereo outputs. It also pans between odd groups (left) and even groups (right) when selected.

5. The channel mute switches off all sends from the channel and so kills that channel completely in all mixes be they pre-fade or post-fade.

6. Routing switches direct the channel signal to selected output groups or the stereo master outputs, in conjunction with the pan control. This example switches the groups in pairs (1&2, 3&4 etc.) larger format console often allow single group routing, in which case the pan control is bypassed.

7. The fader allows precise control of the channel level as it sent to all post fade buses be they auxiliaries or groups.

8. The pfl (pre-fade-listen) button activates the monitoring point where the headphones can be used to listen to the channel in isolation with the applied EQ and any external processing and the signal level can be monitored with a meter. This allows the engineer to hear the exact signal as it lands onto the various mix busses. Selecting several channels is possible but the fader has no effect on the pfl signal. Larger consoles often also allow for afl (after-fade-listen) where the monitoring is taken after the fader.

Fig. 13.4 shows this channel signal path in block form with a little more

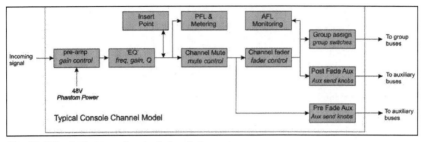

Fig. 13.4 Block diagram of a single input channel.

detail as to the exact signal path. This basic signal path is common to all mixing consoles no matter how big or small though there will be some variations to suite the application.

Insert Point

Fig. 13.4 introduces the insert point which literally allows external signal processing to be inserted into the signal path. In digital consoles this signal processing is probably part of a built-in toolbox of processors, but it could be, as in the analogue world, a physically separate device – see chapter 14.

Groups and Auxiliary Sends

Groups and auxiliary sends differ only in that the groups tend to be switched as shown in fig. 13.5 where each channel is either switched onto the group mix bus or it isn't. Where, as with auxiliary sends, each send is variable as shown in fig. 13.6, allowing different amounts of each channel to be sent to each auxiliary bus. There are some consoles which

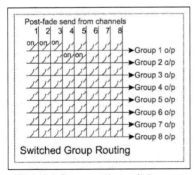

Fig. 13.5 Group routing switches.

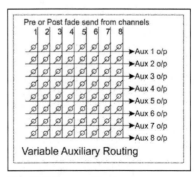

Fig. 13.6 Aux send knobs.

do not differentiate between types of output. An example of this is the smaller format Yamaha digital consoles.

Output Controls

Each of these types of output types (groups, stereo and auxiliaries) needs, at the very least, an output level control as shown in fig. 13.7.
In this example there are:

1. The six auxiliary sends have a level control knob (a) an AFL (after-fade-listen) switch (b) to allow the send to be send to headphones and an overall mute switch (c).

2. There are meters to constantly monitor the main group output levels. The third set will take over the role of channel/auxiliary meter when a channel or auxiliary output is selected to PFL/AFL.

3. These switches allow the groups to operate in sub-group mode which means that they then mix-down to the stereo output when this switch (a) is selected. The stereo output can then be sent to the mono output by using switch (3b).

4. Each output also has a mute switch.

5. Each group has a fader, there is one fader for both sides of the stereo output and the mono output has a fader.

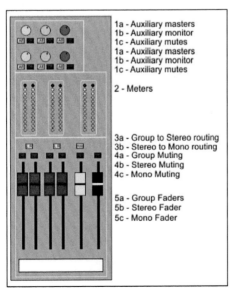

1a - Auxiliary masters
1b - Auxiliary monitor
1c - Auxiliary mutes
1a - Auxiliary masters
1b - Auxiliary monitor
1c - Auxiliary mutes

2 - Meters

3a - Group to Stereo routing
3b - Stereo to Mono routing
4a - Group Muting
4b - Stereo Muting
4c - Mono Muting

5a - Group Faders
5b - Stereo Fader
5c - Mono Fader

Fig. 13.7 Example of a console output section.

Larger format consoles usually have faders for all types of outputs often with full metering for each output, but smaller consoles make cost and space savings by using knobs and using switchable metering.

Matrices

An additional and useful feature found on larger consoles is the matrix. The best way of describing a matrix is to think of it as auxiliary sends from the groups and (usually) the stereo outputs. This allows varying amounts of groups or the stereo to be sent to different parts of the PA system.

Using Sub-Groups and Matrices

Sub Groups allow different sections of the mix to be grouped and controlled and processed together. For example (taking a console with eight sub-groups) you might have one group for all backing vocals, two for a stereo mix of drums, one for main vocals, one for bass guitar and two for a stereo mix of everything else. From

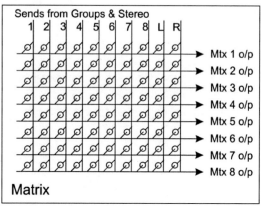

Fig. 13.8 Console Matrix.

here you can decide how to distribute this through the PA by using the matrix. For example if you are using front fills it may be that the rhythm section (drums, bass, etc.) doesn't need to go through the front fills. This could be because the front fills are quite small and not really capable of handling the power. Instead they are there to enhance the vocals and possibly the more melodic parts of the mix. In which case you might set up your sub groups such that you can separate the drums and bass from the vocals and guitar & keyboards; that way you can send everything to the main loudspeakers but bias the front fills to be mainly vocals with some guitar and keyboards and no rhythm. In theatre applications the matrix is a very useful tool for carefully dividing the sends to various parts of the system especially where there is complex shape of venue which requires many different fills for things such as side boxes and under balconies. The key to successfully using a matrix is to ensure that your subgrouping gives you enough control. With larger digital consoles it might be possible to send auxiliaries directly to the matrix too.

Mute Groups

Many consoles offer mute groups which allow you to mute a number of channels from a single button – for example, the entire drum kit, or all the backing vocal mics. Some consoles might offer eight mute groups and others might offer over a hundred mute scenes which are recalled as a list so each song (for example) can have a scene and used mics can be muted to give less background noise and better gain before feedback.

VCAs and DCAs

One other type of control which often confuses new engineers is the VCA (voltage controlled attenuator) often called DCA (digital controlled attenuator) on digital consoles. These are a group of faders which can be assigned to input channels and offer a 'master fader' control for that group. Unlike sub-groups, VCAs/DCAs do not actually have a mix buss that carries audio and so cannot be used as a suitable point to 'insert' any signal processing. What they do is allow you to effectively change the level on a number of channels without actually touching the faders for those channels. These are similar to the mute groups we mentioned above but for faders. And some consoles allow you to define which VCAs/DCAs are assigned to which channel within a programmable list of 'scenes'. Generally VCAs/DCAs do not actually move the channel faders physically but the act as an additional fader in-line with the channel fader. For example if the channel fader is at -10dB and it is assigned to a VCA which is set at -5dB then the total attenuation will be -15dB. Some consoles do have an option to set the VCA/DCA into a mode where the channel faders do move if preferred.

Using PFL and AFL

PFL is a vital tool on the console feature list and anything intended for live use must have such a facility to be any use at all. Each input channel has (or should have) a PFL which has two functions.

Firstly, allow direct monitoring through headphones or a local monitor speaker of the selected channel(s) without affecting the main output(s). The use of a local monitor speaker is very common for stage monitor situations as the monitor engineer can hear exactly what the musician (or other performer) hears through their monitor speaker. The PFL is usually post EQ, but that depends on the console design and some consoles offer the engineer the choice. By its very name the PFL is pre-fader and pre-mute and so can be used to 'pre-view' channels prior to sending them live, which is very handy if you have an off-stage performer who is out of your view and about to come on; you can make sure you don't open the mic to main mix until he/she has finished chatting to the stage crew!

Secondly, allow any channel to be sent to the PFL meter. Even on larger consoles which have a signal meter on each channel, this function is very useful as the PFL meter is usually a larger meter with much higher resolution (more LEDs or a 'real' meter with a needle) and so gives you much more information about the selected channel's behaviour. It is common for one of the main output meters to function as the PFL meter when any PFL button is pressed and then revert back to the output when all PFL buttons are released.

Getting the Mix Right

This is a very big topic which is beyond the scope of this book, but I will just offer a few tips.

The first may seem obvious but like so many techniques it is often forgotten: use your ears. It almost makes me cry when an engineer comes to a virgin console in an unknown venue and starts setting the EQ before he/she has even listened to the system with a CD, let alone with the band playing in a sound check. Admittedly, if the loudspeaker system has been well set up and the band and/or show is well known then initial settings can be made, but always exercise care and be prepared to change preconceived ideas.

Keep it as simple as possible. Use as much processing as is necessary but don't use processing for the sake of it, especially if you are on a short time scale; processing takes time to set up and done badly is will only be detrimental to the overall sound.

As far as possible listen to as much music as possible, whether it is an electronic dance track or a full orchestra; listen to how a good studio mix is built in layers with 'space' in between those layers. It is easy to get all the instruments to the same level and 'fill' the mix, but if you have, for example, two guitars – what are they doing? Is one playing rhythm, in which case it needs to sit in with the bass and drums while the other is carrying something more melodic? In which case use a combination of sensitive level and equalisation to keep them separate in the mix – but be aware that they may swap roles, even within the same song. I use guitars as an example because they are very common in amplified music and yet they can be very difficult to get right especially when you have more than one of them. They can have a very 'fat' sound that covers a vast range of frequencies and as such obliterate everything else around them.

Faders move both ways. It is easy to let a mix 'run away with you' as you push a bit of a solo here and then another there and before you know it the whole mix has crept up to an unmanageable level both in terms of system headroom and gain before feedback. If something is too loud, pull it back, if it has got away, can you pull back the master?

Use your sound check time as efficiently as possible. Test all your mics and find all your faults before you get musicians or performers on stage.

That way you use the musicians to test and fine tune the system and the mix rather than wasting their time getting things working.

Work with your performers and musicians. Many 'old hands' will practically mix themselves; brass players will back-off their mic to 'dim' their sound and keyboard players will play piano (in the original sense of the word meaning *soft*). Talk to the performers and establish what they need and how they usually work and remember that their version of how it should sound may not be the same as yours.

Don't over focus when it comes to the sound check; all too often I see people spend ages on getting the drum kit sounding exactly right and leave no time to get the main vocals right. Keep everything in perspective and be prepared to change your approach as the circumstances change.

14 LINES AND SPLITTERS

Every aspect of live sound involves getting a number of audio signals from several places to several other places and doing something to them in the middle. In many cases the number of signals being moved around is surprisingly large and systems involving hundreds of signals are not uncommon.

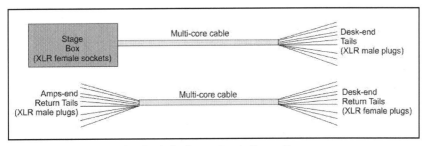

Fig 14.1 Block diagram of a simple tie-line system in live audio.

The basic purpose of the tie-lines or multicore system is to get the signal from the microphones, instruments and any other sources on the stage (or other performance area) to the mixing console and then from the mixing console to the amplifiers. In addition, it is usually necessary to split the feeds from the stages into a second mixing console for stage

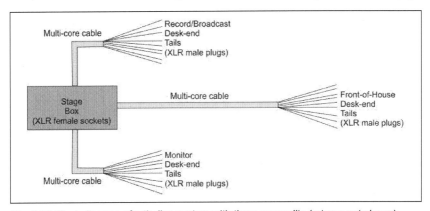

Fig. 14.2 Block diagram of a tie-line system with three way splits (returns not shown).

monitoring, It may also be necessary to take a third split for recording or broadcast as shown in fig. 14.2.

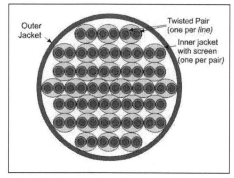

Fig. 14.3 Cross section of typical multicore cable.

There two basic ways of doing this and like mixing consoles they fall into a choice of analogue and digital.

Analogue multicore systems simply use a number of small microphone cables bundled into a single sheath (or jacket), see fig. 14.3, and so behave just like any other microphone cable. The cables can be anything between three or four lines (each line being a single balanced signal, and often called a pair) all the way up to around fifty lines or pairs. For live use most multicores go up to 48 pairs, the limiting factor being the size of the connector and the weight of the cable. If you need more than 48 pairs, then simply run two or more cables.

Digital 'multicore' systems come in a few variations, some being based on generic formats and so are common to a number of manufacturers such as the EtherSound format used in the Yamaha ES168-SB, whilst others are proprietary and locked to a certain manufacturer such as the Roland Digital Snake system. Digital line systems take the analogue source signals, then convert them into the digital domain, multiplex them (that is make lots of signals fit down one cable) then transmit that digital multiplexed signal to the other end where it is de-multiplexed (that is the multiplexed signal is all divided back into the individual signals) and either converted back into analogue signals or fed directly into the digital mixing console.

Inevitably there are advantages and disadvantages to both systems:

Analogue Advantages

- Simple and easy to use.
- No compatibility issues, can be used with any console.
- Can carry signals either way.
- No power required at either end.
- Can be used for non-audio signals such as communication systems (coms) and cue-lights.

- Minor damage can be tolerated – one or two broken lines (perhaps due one or two broken pins on the connector) don't prevent you using the rest of the lines.

Analogue Disadvantages
- High frequency signal loss – especially over longer distances. The 'capacitive' cable attenuates the high frequencies, the longer the cable the worse the problem.
- Weight – 100m of 48 pair cable with connectors is likely to over 100kg and that excludes the drum and flight case.

Digital Advantages
- Lightweight often using a single cat5/cat6 cable, coaxial cable or fibre-optic where 100m easily fits onto a small drum.
- Large capacity systems of 64 channels or more can be carried over a single small cable.
- Lossless. Some systems support runs of over 1km with no progressive loss of high frequencies but this does depend on high quality analogue to digital (A to D) conversion.
- Often incorporated into the console system makes splits and patch set up much simpler as it is all done in the console(s) rather than in masses of stage-side spaghetti.

Digital Disadvantages
- Can only carry audio signals – not suitable for things such as comms and cue-lights.
- Some systems can be a bit fiddly to set up so make sure you are familiar with them and any set-up software you might need before your event.
- Can only carry signals one way. Often they are arranged with a number of sends (from stage to console) and a number of returns (from console back to stage). These numbers are fixed so if you have (for example) a 32 send, eight returns you can't simply add a ninth return and reduce the sends to 31, which you can with an analogue system.
- Compatibility – system types cannot be mixed without breaking out of the digital domain into analogue and back again or using third party conversion boxes which are only available for certain types of system.
- Damage to a single cable can kill all the signals that cable carries. However the cable is usually very cheap in comparison to comparable multicore so always carry (and run) more than you need.

Digital Latency
I have stayed away from the thorny topic of digital latency as I believe it

to be a much maligned phenomena that, if correctly managed, is of no consequence on the live stage. In this context Latency refers to the time delay caused by the analogue signal being digitised and digital signals being processed. Any system which used analogue to digital or digital to analogue (A to D or D to A) conversion or Digital Signal Processing will introduce a small amount of delay – usually in the order of around a few thousandths (or less) of a second. These time delays are insignificant when compared to the time it takes the acoustic sound to propagate through the air. They only become significant (and sometimes quite nasty) when singles are mixed together with different amounts of delay. The key to managing latency is to ensure that all signals have the same latency and that the latency is kept below a few ms (milliseconds). One of the best ways to do this is to avoid crossing the digital-analogue line too often: once you're in the digital domain stay there if you can.

Which System to Use

If you have an analogue console and your cable lengths can be kept below 50m or so, then often the simplest way is to stay in the analogue domain as this probably gives most flexibility. However the cost and weight savings of a simple cat5 cable based digital system cannot be over-looked and the digital solution can be employed, but it is good practice to run a small (say eight-pair or fewer) analogue cable alongside this so that comms, talk-back mics and other similar things can be run easily.

On the other had if you have a digital console with an integral lines system, then make the best of it. I often see (and with good reason as it makes good sense) hybrid systems with a 'main' digital stage box system that handle the long runs to FOH and the split to monitors with small eight or 12 pair 'satellite' multicores that are often just a simple box with 10m or more of multicore cable and a set of tails. It makes good sense to try

Source	Mic	Sub-Core	Main Core	FOH Chan	Mon Chan	Notes
Kick Drum	D112	Red 1	1	1	1	
Snare	SM57	Red 2	2	2	2	
. . .						
. . . .						
. . . . .						
Saxphone	Own Radio Sys		33	20	22	864.1MHz
. . .						
. . . .						
. . . . .						
Keys 1 Left	AR133 DI	Blue 1	24	11	15	
Keys 1 Right	AR133 DI	Blue 2	25	12	16	
Keys 2 Left	AR133 DI	Blue 3	26	13	17	
Keys 2 Right	AR133 DI	Blue 4	27	14	18	·

Fig. 14.4 Sample patch sheet for use on stage.

and use satellite systems were possible, usually where a number of mics are grouped together on a drum kit or string section for example as it reduces the number of individual cables crossing the stage and makes the whole thing neater.

One of the most important things is to help the whole event to run smoothly is to keep clear notes of how signals are distributed. Fig.14.4 shows an example of this. If the event is well rehearsed then, as shown here, the data can be typed up and printed off. Otherwise a simple blank grid can be created and laminated to allow it to be written on with a suitable marker pen. The lamination also makes it resistant to rain (outdoor gigs) or coffee and drinking water (all gigs).

Split Systems

There are a number of ways of achieving a viable split system for the stage microphone feeds:

- Simple wired split
- Passive transformer split
- Fully active split
- Split with digital domain

The simple wired split involves just wiring the same microphone to both the front-of-hose (PA) mixer feeds and the Monitor console feeds in parallel as in fig. 14.5. This method is cheap and effective but if there as a short circuit fault on the line feed to one console then the other console will lose the signal too. In addition any re-plugging at one console is likely to cause clicks and bangs on the signal feeding the other console. In addition this simple system can be a source of noise through earth-loops and other induced noise problems. This method is definitely not recommended for situations where more than two splits are required.

The passive transformer[1] split system goes some way to solving this, an example is shown in fig. 14.6. By transformer isolating the various feeds noise is less easily transmitted to one console by patching or other similar activates at the other; the transformer removes most of the possible causes of induced noise. There are various ways of wiring transformer splits and this is just one example. A short circuit on either

---

1   Transformers work by turning electrical signals into magnetic ones and turning these magnetic signals back into electrical ones. They do this in a very confined and controlled way and with very high degrees of efficiency. The result is that there is no direct electrical connection between the input and the output and, when used with correctly balanced signals their noise rejection ability is unsurpassed.

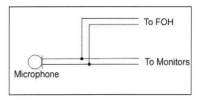

Fig. 14.5 Simple wired split.

the record or monitor outputs will reduce the levels but not kill the line altogether. For these reasons, this can be employed in three way split systems for broadcast or recording feeds.

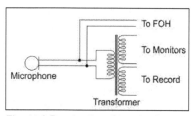

Fig. 14.6 Passive transformer split system example.

The next and most expensive option on the analogue domain is the active split system which uses a line amplifier to achieve lossless splits with maximum isolation and noise immunity.

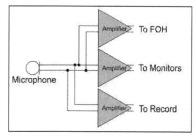

Fig. 14.7 Active split example.

Active splits, like passive, can be configured in a number of ways. The example in fig. 14.7 shows a purely electronic version but a number of commercial products offer transformer coupling on some outputs and electronic coupling on other outputs.

15 SIGNAL PROCESSING

Although nearly every item we have discussed so far processes a signal in some form or another, the term signal processing generally refers to a device which allows us to alter the signal in some creative way. There is a bewildering array of devices out there and this book can't hope to give you an in depth guide to them but they can usually be broken down into three basic categories:

- Equalisers
- Dynamic Processors
- Effects Processors

Equalisers

Equalisation allows parts of the frequency spectrum to be cut (attenuated or reduced in level) or boosted (amplified or increased in level). We looked briefly at this in the section on controlling feedback for stage monitors. Each and every console channel has some equalisation on it and each and every loudspeaker system will use some equalisation to get the output of the loudspeaker frequency response to be as flat as possible. Equalisers mean we can add more 'punch' to drums by boosting low and/or low-midrange frequencies. They can give an electric guitar a more aggressive 'edge' by boosting high-mid-range frequencies. Equalisers can give more clarity to a voice by reducing lower and often resonant frequencies.

Typically equalisers fall into two categories: graphic and parametric. Graphic equalisers use a number of bands of fixed width controlled by a line of faders which graph out the alterations made to the frequency spectrum as these faders are moved. These faders are usually half-octave spaced (16 faders) or third-octave spaced (32 faders).

Fig. 15.1 shows typical frequency bands and the arrangement of faders. This sample shows a cut at 308Hz and a wider cut from 1kHz to 1.25kHz and a boost between 4kHz and 8kHz. This would give us the modified frequency output shown in fig. 15.2.

Fig. 15.1 32 band graphic equaliser.

Such equalisers can either be a sequence of analogue filters

Fig. 15.2 Result of the graphic equaliser settings.

or they could be incorporated into a digital signal processor (DSP). They could even be included into a processing library in a digital mixing console. However, they are presented, they all operate in the same way. Graphic equalisers give an easy user interface and allow us to boost and cut anywhere in the frequency band that we choose and the effects are easy to tune by ear to suit our objectives. However, they can be rather blunt instruments as each of the filters is fixed width and when considering digital signal processing (DSP) resources all those filters can be rather inefficient depending on how the manufacturer has implemented them as it may be that even the unused filters are taking processing resources.

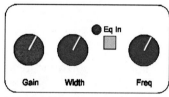

Fig. 15.3 Typical parametric equaliser controls.

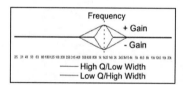

Fig. 15.4 Result of parametric equaliser settings.-

The alternative is the parametric equaliser. Parametric equalisers usually have three controls per band: frequency, Q (or width) and gain as shown in fig. 15.3.

The frequency control selects the centre frequency to adjust, the Q selects the range (or width) of the adjustment and the gain selects the amount of cut of boost. Do check how the Width knob is scaled as some equalisers use the term Q instead but technically higher Q filters focus on a narrower band so it is not unusual to have one type of parametric equaliser to adjust a wider range of frequencies as the knob is turned clockwise while another equaliser may work the other way and adjust a narrower range as the knob is turned the same way. This type of equaliser is perhaps harder to use and needs a bit more thought than a graphic equaliser, but it gives the user a much more accurate tool allowing very precise adjustments or gentle sweeping contours as required. All reasonable console channels feature this type of equalisation.

The best way to get a feel for equaliser is to use them. Start with a favourite music CD and see what happens as you change the settings. Look back at Fig. 2.2 and note how the various instruments and voices shown there fit into the frequency spectrum. You'll see that the fundamentals (the basis of the notes) fit well into the left hand side of the equaliser. Most of the right hand side is the harmonics. A sample CD of various solo instruments can be a good tool to getting to know equalisers too.

In larger systems it is usual to have different equalisers assigned to different roles. We have already seen the system controller equaliser used to flatten the loudspeaker response curve and additional resources in such processors can be used to flatten the room response. Such careful correction may be done with audio analysers or just careful listening, but either way it is best left alone when the heat of the soundcheck arrives unless some systemic problem (such as every microphone ringing at the same frequency) becomes apparent. For this reason channel or group EQ (be it on the channel itself or inserted internally or externally) is the best place to go.

Dynamic Processors

Dynamic Processors actively control the level of a signal in some way. For example, compressors attenuate a signal when it goes above a set threshold. Thereafter the level is reduced proportionately by a set ratio. Gates are used to switch a signal on when it reaches a set threshold and were originally intended to keep out background noise by only opening when the signal was high enough. However they are frequently used to make percussion more punchy keeping the microphone signal clean by only turning the channel on when the drum in question is hit and a sufficiently large signal passes into the microphone. By effectively muting the microphone the rest of the time there is less unwanted noise through the system and the mix can be kept cleaner. Expanders are gates with the ability to set how much off to use. So compressors reduce the dynamic range of a signal – that is the difference between its loudest and quietest parts are reduced. Gates and expanders increase the dynamic range of signals.

There is a hybrid between dynamic processors and equalisers which apply dynamic processing (compressing and expansion) to selected parts of the frequency spectrum rather that to entire range. This allows (for example) vocal resonance or sibilance to be controlled by compressing the problem frequencies.

Effects Processors

Whereas the other two categories of processing simply apply variations or control the existing signal, effects processors actually add something to the sound. The most common of those is the reverb processor although these are now usually built into some kind of multi-effects processor.

Reverberation Processors use various digital algorithms to mimic the reverberation of concert halls and other performance spaces. There is a large range of complexity (and price) and the only way to judge them is to try them out. Many of the more complex (and more costly) ones have too many parameters available for the live engineer who rarely has the time to fine tune the effect in the way a studio engineer has; most of the time a good Concert Hall setting will suffice. This can be fine-tuned using the early reflection time and the reverb time:

- Early reflection time defines the size of the room – too long and a cavernous effect is created, too short and a boxy 'small room' sound is created.
- The reverb time is really the amount of reverb that is added. This is effectively how reflective the walls are in your virtual space.

By all means find a unit you like the sound of and explore all the parameters you can, but I suspect that like most of us you will eventually come down to three or four different versions of your favourite preset.

Many of the other effects available in multi effect processors like flange, phase, etc. are musician's tools and should only be employed if requested by a musician for a specific effect, though of course you can always make suggestions.

16 GAIN STRUCTURE

Gain structure is another often misunderstood term; it is often thought to be a highly complex topic involving maths and calculators, but actually it is very simple. However, simple as it may be, it is also vitally important to get it right – and contrary to another often held misconception it is even more vital to get it right in digital systems than in purely analogue ones.

Basically, gain structure describes the changing level of the signal as it passes through the audio system from the lowest levels in microphones and instruments (being thousandths of volts) to the highest levels in loudspeakers (which can be hundreds of volts similar to that present in a mains wall outlet) and the various amplification stages (level increase) and attenuation stages (level decrease) necessary to achieve the correct output for the desired application. If the gain is badly structured, then the results could be noisy, distorted or both and in the worst case could be noisy and distorted and then not actually loud enough. In the digital domain poor gain structure leads to either the brutal distortion that is known as digital clip or at the other end of the scale, inaccurate sampling which can cause more subtle problems such as unexciting sound due to inadequate bit depth; at lower level the digital encoding becomes less precise and the quality reduction is all too apparent.

The fastest way to optimise the gain structure is to ensure that every piece of equipment has a healthy incoming signal – and for this, equipment with good metering is essential. Often budget equipment scrimps on the metering and that is usually its downfall. So, if you have a dynamic microphone connected the input channel of your console, you might turn your gain control up to about 43dB. The aim should be to get a healthy pre-fade meter level of around 0dB. Obviously if you have a quiet vocalist on this mic you might need more gain than if the same mic were doing a pair of bongos or an energetic trombonist! Don't forget to allow for the dynamic range of the thing that the microphone is picking up; you don't want the loudest sound the thing is capable of generating driving the input channel into distortion (or clip), so it may be that most of the time the channel is hovering around -10dB or lower as you know that once or twice in the show the singer or instrumentalist gives it some 'welly' and pushes the level up to +10dB or higher! This should ensure that any 'inserted' signal processing gets an acceptable range of signals and that the console (be it analogue or digital) is working in its optimum range. By maintaining this optimum level throughout the console as we move the signal through group and auxiliary buses and through any additional processing to the console outputs (maybe via a matrix) and on to the loudspeaker processors (if required) and amplifiers then we are ensuring that all this equipment is also working in its optimum range. With this in mind all your faders should be around the 0dB mark too. If this means your system is too loud then ultimately the best way to reduce the level is at the input to the loudspeaker processor (or for more simple passive systems, at the amplifier itself). This ensures the maximum signal to noise ratio and the lowest quiescent noise floor.

In the example shown in fig. 16.1, the dynamic ranges of various sections of the signal path are shown as a broad grey line within which variations of a microphone signal are illustrated by a solid white, a black line and a dotted white line as they are adjusted as they pass

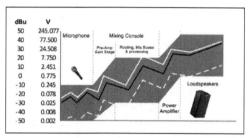

Fig. 16.1 Gain processing within a system.

through the system. The black line remains comfortably within range at all times but the solid white line is boosted too far at some point in the latter part of the console (perhaps the fader is pushed too far up with the gain set too high) and will distort (clip).

The dotted white line on the other hand drops below the 'noise floor' so the signal falls below the level that the console can reproduce and noise (usually a hiss but also have some buzzing in it) becomes the dominant component of the signal instead of the voice or instrument that we wanted. So keeping the gain structure on track is essential to high quality sound.

When it comes to setting up your overall system level, the final level must be set at the amplifiers (or the crossover-controllers); that way everything before can bet set to optimum gain and the final control is then defined at the end of the signal chain.

17 FAULT FINDING

One of the best skills that a live sound engineer can possess is the ability to quickly diagnose and rectify problems. Every event will throw up problems and faults that will stand in the way of achieving the objective of giving the audience the best possible sound for every seat in the house. The more time spent dealing with problems, the less time there is available to get on with sound checks and polishing the result. A cool and level headed approach to finding and dealing with these problems is essential. For the purposes of discussion I have separated faults on the input side of the mixing console from output faults as there are differences that can be applied.

Common input faults include:

- Input channel not working – no signal from microphone appearing at console input.
- Weak or 'thin' sound from an input channel.
- Excessive noise on an input channel.
- Distorted sound from an input channel.

Common output faults include:

- Output not working – signal not coming out of loudspeaker when it is expected to.
- Weak or 'thin' sound on output channel.
- Excessive noise on an output channel.
- Distorted sound on an output channel.

Input Channel Faults

Channel not working

If you have a completely dead input channel, that is one with a microphone (or other source) plugged into it and yet nothing appears on the channel meter nor can you hear anything on the PFL. Exactly how you find such a fault depends on the complexity of your system and the amount of walking needed between stage and console but here is one possible sequence. The important thing is to be methodical and only change one thing at a time.

1. Check the obvious first. All these are done from behind the console and so are pretty quick to do.

    b. Are you sure your headphones (or other local listening device is working properly). For example if you have tested some channels already and then one doesn't work then the PFL is OK but have you stepped on your head phone lead? These points sound might seem blindingly obvious but I, like many, have sent an assistant off on a wild-goose chase only to find out that the headphone jack has come out of the console.

    c. If the microphone (or other source) needs phantom power, is it switched on?

    d. Is there a piece of faulty or miswired outboard equipment inserted into the channel? Many PFLs take their signal after the insert point to allow the processing to be heard.

    e. Does the console have switchable inputs and if so is the correct one selected. For example some consoles use a second (often ¼" jack) connector for the line input option so make sure you have selected the correct input.

    f. Does the console have a 'soft patch' whereby physical sockets can be connected to any channel(s), for example input socket 15 might be soft-patched to channel 10. This is only applicable on digital consoles.

2. Work systematically along the signal chain. I have chosen to go from the microphone back to the mixer but the other way might be equally valid.

    a. Is the microphone (or other source) plugged in? In the spaghetti-cable-situation that often exists in the set-up phase of any event, make sure that the mic is plugged into the right line.

    b. Try a different and preferably previously tested (and known to be working) microphone. If the microphone requires phantom power, try a dynamic microphone which does not. If that works you can test for phantom power with a multimeter (see fig. 16.1) or other phantom power testing device.

    c. If it still doesn't work, try replacing the cable.

    d. If possible try a different multicore line. This will mean changing the patch at the stage end and the console end. If you are using a splits system, try a different channel of that.

    e. Eventually you come back to plugging a microphone directly into the desk channel and if it still doesn't work you have a dead desk channel so re-patch and start again.

Hopefully you will discover a simple wiring or patching fault is the cause of your trouble. Nearly all such faults come down to a damaged cable or damaged connector – especially the small pins used in multicore systems. If you can't simply replace the cable then patch around it and move on. Take care to mark the faulty equipment so that whoever is responsible for checking it after the event can get it fixed before it is next needed and so that nobody else picks it up and tries to use it on this event.

To test phantom power in a mic line:

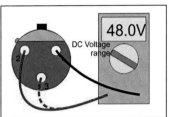

Fig. 17.1 Using a multimeter to test phantom power.

- Make sure the phantom power is applied to the microphone input in question.
- Set your multimeter to the 50Vdc range (or nearest higher range).
- Insert the black probe into socket 1
- Insert the red probe into socket 2 and read the voltage.
- Insert the red probe into socket 3 and read the voltage.

Both sockets 2 and 3 should give you around +48V dc with respect to socket 1.If either give you 0 or some other low value you probably have a broken cable somewhere along the line. If both 2 and 3 give you a zero or low value then either the console (or other phantom power providing device) isn't providing the phantom power or the screen on pin/socket 1 is broken. If you get unbalanced values then the most likely cause is the console (or whatever is providing the phantom power). Using a multimeter to test phantom power in this way is a good way of proving all three wires in the balanced line cable.

The small pins used in multicore connector are notorious for getting slightly bent or pushed back into the pin-bed which can cause connections to fail or in rare cases to short against adjacent pins.

Weak or thin sound

A weak or thin sound is usually caused either by a faulty microphone or by a broken wire along the line. If a microphone is dropped, sometimes the diaphragm can get damaged or detached which restricts its movement and the sound is badly compromised. A broken wire means that the balanced line is no longer effective and a weak and often very noisy sound is the result. The test process is (or can be) identical to that for a non-working channel but this time you are listening for the signal to suddenly improve when you bypass the faulty part of the system. Don't forget to check that you haven't got any processing inserted onto the channel such as a severe EQ that has been 'left over' from a previous job.

Excessive Noise

Excessive noise can be a faulty wire which prevents the balanced input stage from working properly especially if a weak or thin sound is heard. Or it could be a broken screen (pin 1) however in the case of phantom powered devices, this would stop them working altogether but you might still get a buzzing noise. If this seems to be the case use the method described above to work through and try to find the point at which the noise disappears. Otherwise listen to the noise and try to establish what causes it.

A low 50Hz distorted buzzing (60Hz in the USA) is indicative of mains noise: is the microphone or its cable close to heavy power consumers like motor controllers or dimmer racks?

Is the noise acoustic caused by a smoke machine or other piece of noisy stage hardware that might have 'appeared' after you carefully positioned the microphone?

If the noise is a higher pitched sizzling noise, the chances are it comes from an electronic power supply of the type used in laptops, etc. Is the buzzing line fed by a laptop acting as a software instrument or backing track player? In which case look at how you have connected the item to your mixer: would a DI box help and in this case the electronic ones often provide more options than the simpler passive ones. Make sure the output of the device is running as hard as it can and without distorting, that way if you turn it down at the console, you'll turn the noise down too.

Distorted input

Distorted sound that is also weak is most likely a cable fault, a microphone fault, a desk fault, or that rogue piece of processing equipment again. As with all such faults, double check the obvious things at the desk then work along the line fault-finding as you go. Cable shorts are often caused by crushed cables breaking down the insulation between the conductors which causes short-circuits that can lead to distorted sound. Sometimes a phantom power fault (which can be caused by such a short) means that the supply voltage drops significantly and the microphone or DI box tries its best but ultimately fails to deliver.

Output Faults

There are slightly different techniques that can be adopted for finding output faults, and one of the most useful is that the line output from a console or other audio device is strong enough to directly drive a pair of headphones. With some practice the tip and ring from a stereo ¼" jack can be held against pins 2 & 3 of a male (output) XLR connector. This allows you hear the line output. If you want you can buy or make an adaptor cable to connect your headphones to the line. In this case it is best to remove the connection to pin 1 because:

1. You avoid applying phantom power to your headphones. In practice this is unlikely but can be damaging to both your headphones and your ears if you do!

2. You avoid the possibility of connecting your headphones to a loudspeaker line. XLRs should NEVER be used for loudspeakers especially with the output being on pins (male connector), but there is still some equipment out there where this is the case and they are usually just wired to pins 1 & 2. Obviously you don't want to connect your headphones to the output of a power amp as damage to headphones and your ears is a high probability!

3. The downside is that unbalanced lines that just use pins 1 & 2 cannot be monitored in this way, so you have to just hold the headphone jack in place.

Take note of point 1 and never connect your headphones to any line that you suspect might have phantom power on (which usually runs between pins 2 & 3 at +48V and pin 1 at 0V). And never connect your headphones to the output of a large power amplifier.

With these cautionary words in mind you now have a very useful field diagnostic tool as you can monitor a known signal to the point of failure. For example, if you have a feed (to a loudspeaker or recorder for example) that isn't working, then start at the source (usually the mixing console output) and work your way down the line. Send a known audio signal to the console output (such as a tone generator or CD player), if you can monitor the source at the output then the console is working OK. So move onto the next thing in the line – this could be a single cable or a complex patching system. Either way, as with input fault-finding, be methodical and when you lose the signal you know that the fault lies between where you are now and the last place you found to be working. If you had a signal going into a cable and not coming out of the other end, change the cable. If you find a faulty line in a multicore system, use a different line.

Either way, if you do find a fault in a cable or other device, always mark it with a meaningful description and ensure that nobody else tries to use it until it gets repaired.

If you don't have a pair of headphones to hand you can use a robust dynamic mic such as an SM58 – though you will need an XLR female-female adaptor to connect its male connector to the line output's male connector. The desk line output will generate a very thin tinny sound from the microphone, but it can be useful in an emergency.

As for the list of common faults, the same basic principles apply as for input fault finding. So before the power amplifiers:

- Check the obvious things first: is the output enabled on the console, is it unmuted, is it sending an output, is it soft-patched correctyl (is the physical input you want being routed to the correct control channel).
- Check for faulty or incorrectly set-up processing equipment.
- Look for cable faults by swapping out or using the headphone test described above.
- Weak and thin sound often points to faulty or incorrect equipment settings or a broken wire in a cable.
- Excessive noise could be poor gain structure, faulty equipment or a broken screen in a cable.
- Distortion could be poor gain structure, faulty equipment or a shorting cable.

And after the power amplifiers the options get rather more simple as anything is either going to be:

- An incorrectly set or faulty amplifier.
- A loudspeaker cable fault.
- A loudspeaker fault.

The key is again to be methodical. Loudspeaker faults can be very time consuming to fix so it is a good (if not essential) idea to test them before they are put into place, even if it is just a CD player straight into the back of an amplifier and listen to each cabinet in turn to ensure that all the components (high frequency driver, mid frequency driver, etc.) are working. Listen for unusual sound and buzzes and rattles that might interfere with satisfactory operation. Any faults found at this stage will be far easier to fix than when the array is suspended 10m in the air! Don't forget to test the loudspeakers AND the feeder cables which will be suspended with the array as you don't want to have to climb up to the array to fix a broken cable either.

If you do this you should be in a position where there are no loudspeaker faults that you haven't already found and your fault finding becomes simpler.

Earth (Ground) Loops

If you find that you have an unacceptable low buzz (50Hz plus harmonics or 60Hz for the USA) and you cannot localise it to one microphone or other piece of equipment, then you might have an earth loop. If you can trace it to one item of equipment then it might be that that item is creating an earth loop. The mains (50Hz or 60Hz) component of an earth loop is usually the most prominent but with high frequency switching power supplies and computer clock oscillators ever more common in equipment, don't be surprised by high frequency whines be an indicator of earth loops too.

What is an Earth Loop

An earth loop is basically an aerial that is created when your audio system has two (or more) signal earth points and a reasonable high impedance loop between them. This has the effect of picking up any induced noise that happens to be in the area – and a strong 50Hz electromagnetic interference cause by power cables fits nicely! Because the impedance of the loop is high relatively, then the noise is not simply transmitted to earth and disappears as would be intended. Instead the signal ground, which is the reference point for the entire system is modulated by the noise and so it finds its way into the signal. At its worst every single signal path can be modulated in this way and the whole system buzzes. In other situations it might just be limited to a single input channel resulting from some poor piece of backline equipment that a musician happened to bring along.

The solution is, like so many, to limit the possibility of such a situation ever arising in the first place; to limit the number of signal earth points in a system. Thise does not mean removing any mains supply earths! Mains earths (the green or green and yellow wire in the plug) are there for reasons of electrical safety and should never be disconnected. The problem will lie in how the signal earth relates to the mains earth and sometimes removing the pin 1 link from the XLR cable into a piece of equipment removes a current path through which an induced noise current can modulate the ground on that piece of equipment. A number of short cables or in-line couplers (clearly marked) in your cables kit which only have pins 2 and 3 wired are a handy way to test and possibly eliminate one earth-loop problem. Other solutions include using signal-transformers to remove any direct connection between equipment and thus removing any unwanted current paths. A useful addition to anybody's tool kit is a selection of balancing transformer boxes (600Ω for line transmission and 10kΩ for line reception) with switches choose to link the earth through or not. Beware of cheaper transformers which might offer poor bandwidth (poor low and/or high frequency response) or distort well below +20du.

DI boxes can help too especially with noisy instrument and backline problems. Most DI boxes have transformers and earth isolation switches in them for this reason.

All hum and noise problems depend on the environment you are in at the time. This environment includes the exact configuration of balanced to unbalanced wiring, the quality of the input and output stages, how much noise there is around (which depends on mains cable positioning and loading and other noise producing devices), how long the interconnections are and the gain structure of the system.

Sometime you might hear about bad mains being the cause of the noise; this is highly unlikely. That said, there can be situations when the mains supply voltage falls so low that the power supplies inside equipment can't deliver the voltage required and that will cause all sorts of problems – noise being just one of them. If you suspect there is a mains problem, get a reading of the mains voltage at load end of the cable under load. If it is within 8% then most likely that isn't your problem. Some equipment even gives tolerances as wide as 20% or more.

Earth faults on power distribution systems or cables can also be a cause but these should be regularly checked for safety reasons as the potential to kill somebody is rather more serious than a buzz on a sound system! The chopped waveforms thrown out by dimmers and motor controllers can cause noise problems but these are much more likely to EMI be (electromagnetic interference) radiated from dimmers, inverters, cables, motors and lamps and picked up by your earth loops than carried into your equipment by the mains feed.

Test Equipment

You can spend a great deal of money and carry a considerable weight in test equipment, but at the basic level the test equipment in your toolbox must include:

- A reasonable multimeter
- A reasonable Sound Pressure Meter
- A good pair of headphones
- A dynamic microphone

If you work with radio microphones then a small frequency scanner allows you to hear the signal directly out of the transmitter.

A laptop is becoming standard equipment as many devices use software control interfaces to facilitate easy set and group control. In addition there are excellent analytical tools such as SMAART to aid system set up in a Real Time Analysis capacity. And then you can also use it as a media player or multitrack recorder when you're backed into a corner and you have a suitable converter. Similar apps are available for iPad and other tablet platforms.

Phase (Polarity) Checkers

One additional tool that is of immense use is the phase checker. It can save many hours chasing odd system behaviour and strange effects that are caused by simple wiring faults or basic incorrect system settings. In the case of faulty wiring, the time saving can be massive if the only cure is to get the riggers out of the pub and send them up the truss the replace one cable with a +/- cross connection.

Phase Delay and Polarity

These things and their names are very often a source of confusion and misinformation in the audio industry. All too often the Φ symbol is used on a piece of equipment to signify a polarity reversal (effectively + becomes - and - becomes +) which has very little to do with true phase issues:

- Phase is specified in either degrees or radians and is a fraction of a complete cycle (one cycle being 360° or 2π radians) and so there is a relationship between phase and delay which is dependent on frequency and time
- Delay is specified in milliseconds (although feet or meters are sometimes used too) which is independent of frequency
- Polarity is either right or wrong – hence phase reverse switches only have two positions!

Despite these differences, the two terms phase and polarity are very often interchanged. This leads to such phrases as phase inversion and polarity inversion or phase reversal and polarity reversal actually meaning the same thing. In practice a 180°phase shift is a reversal of polarity, provided that it occurs across the whole bandwidth in question. True phase problems however are much more subtle and they are the subject of a whole different discussion. In this article I will, out of respect for convention, use the term phase reverse in the strictly incorrect context that it has come to mean.

How a Phase Checker Works

Most phase checkers come as two separate boxes – a pulse generator and a pulse detector. The PC80 product form LA Audio is typical example but there are many similar units on the market. They usually come in two boxes: a pulse generator with a line output socket and a detector with a line input socket and often an internal microphone with a red and a green led to show the test result. Both units are usually switchable between pin 2 and pin 3 hot on the XLR connectors to allow for unbalanced connection systems.

The pulse generator produces a pulse wave which looks something like fig 17.2.

This pulse is fed into the system under test and the output is fed into the detector which looks at the polarity of the pulse it receives. If it receives the same polarity of pulse then it shows a green led fig. 17.3. If it sees a pulse that looks more like fig 17.4 then it will show a red LED.

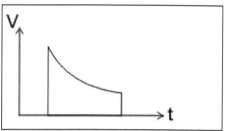

Fig 17.2 Phase checker pulse waveform

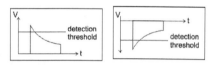

Fig 17.3 Positive pulse detection   *Fig 17.4 Negative pulse detection*

In practice the pulse gets chewed up by filters as well as loudspeaker responses but the critical bit is the leading edge crossing the detection threshold – positive going shows green, negative shows red.

Using a Phase Checker

Fig 17.5 is a typical way to connect a phase checker to test a loudspeaker system.

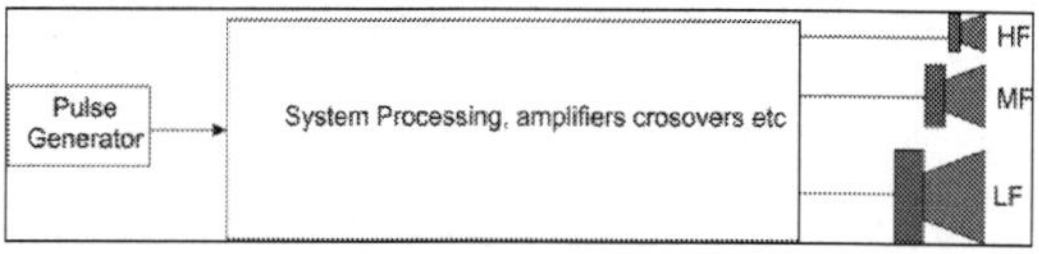

Since the detector is a fairly simple soul and

Fig 17.5

simply detects the polarity of the first pulse above its detection threshold so it is important not to confuse it by feeding it pulses from multiple sources at the same time; as far as possible test only one unit at a time - mute or disconnect everything else. This way you can quickly run through the system one box at a time. Ideally you would test your system in this way as you 'flash' through it before flying it. That way cable faults can be corrected more easily.

Typical results are shown in fig 17.6

Fig 17.6 HF shows red, the rest give green

There are many reasons why different components in a loudspeaker system might be deliberately set out of phase: such as compensation for time alignment between

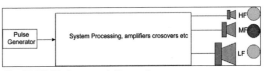

Fig 17.7 MF shows red, the rest green

horns and direct radiating drivers, compensation for crossover distortion. It is very common for a pulse-phase-checker (such as this) to give a green light on the mid-range and a red light on the HF, as shown in fig 17.6; this is not necessarily wrong. The best solution is to get to know the system you are using and if you don't, compare like for like; if there is one box that gives a different result from all the others there is a problem that needs investigating.

For example if all but one of your loudspeaker systems shows the results above and one shows as fig 17.7 then look at any of these possible points:

1. An incorrect processor or crossover setting
2. A cable fault between processor or crossover and amplifier
3. An amplifier with a 'pin 3 hot input' or miswired output terminals
4. A cable fault between amplifier and loudspeaker
5. A loudspeaker driver wired incorrectly in the cabinet

Obviously the number of sections of your system that show a particular fault can help you diagnose the problem: if all the speakers fed from one amplifier display the same symptoms then the fault lies in or before that amplifier, if all the speakers 'downstream' from a particular cable display the same

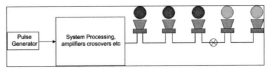

Fig 17.8 Five speakers with two potential wiring faults

symptoms then look at that cable. You might even get compound faults such as the system of linked speakers shown in fig 17.8 where a mis-wired amplifier introduces a phase reversal which is then corrected by a miswired link cable.

Interpreting the Results

Generally speaking the lower the frequency (and so the longer the wavelength) the more noticeable phase problems will be. This is because the physical positioning of sources and reflective boundaries will be fractions of wavelengths apart and thus cause the most cancellation effects. So as far as possible - and this is especially important when you are mixing non-identical speaker systems – try to get your subs in phase first and then work up through your frequency range. Good manufacturers should maintain a characteristic approach to system design so that any sub can be used with any hi-mid cabinet.

As you move up through the frequency range polarity reversals within systems are common to compensate for many real-world problems in loudspeaker cabinet design both in active and passive systems which are far too subtle for a simple pulse generator/detector system to measure. However higher frequencies contribute much more to your sense if imaging - which is why you should always use identical left and right systems in critical applications. For this reason I would always advocate sourcing as much of you system as possible from the same manufacturer and one with a sensible approach to phase response for those critical applications.

Good Practice

Provided the following advice is adhered to, most phase checkers should give consistent results when testing identical loudspeaker systems:

1. All systems being compared must be driven at exactly the same level. Just to be sure, check one system first to see whether the chosen volume lies at a "critical" level, i.e. whether a phase jump takes place just above or below the selected volume level

2. The detector should be placed in exactly the same place relative to the drivers and directly on the front grill of each loudspeaker, as close as possible to the centre of the driver, and under no circumstances in front of the reflex port(s).

3. Loudspeakers should be tested singly (i.e. one at a time) with others turned off especially in arrays or any large clusters of subwoofers.

If a phase checker gives confusing readings and a reference system isn't available, then a spectrum analyser plus noise generator can be of assistance with full-range systems. If drivers within one cabinet are polarity reversed, an audible hole will be seen in the crossover region. Of course you won't know whether it's the HF or LF driver which is reversed until further investigation has been done.

Phase reversals are most commonly found in the wiring of the cables of the signal chain.

Apart from checking loudspeaker polarity, and provided active crossovers, equalisers and effects units are excluded, a phase checker will normally provide correct and consistent indication of a polarity reversal in the signal chain.

ENTERTAINMENT TECHNOLOGY PRESS

FREE SUBSCRIPTION SERVICE

Keeping Up To Date with

Introduction to live Sound

Entertainment Technology titles are continually up-dated, and all major changes and additions are listed in date order in the relevant dedicated area of the publisher's website. Simply go to the front page of www.etnow.com and click on the BOOKS button. From there you can locate the title and be connected through to the latest information and services related to the publication.

The author of the title welcomes comments and suggestions about the book and can be contacted by email at:
roland@rolandhigham.co.uk

Titles Published by Entertainment Technology Press

50 Rigging Calls *Chris Higgs, Cristiano Giavedoni 246pp* **£16.95**
ISBN: 9781904031758
Chris Higgs, author of ETP's two leading titles on rigging, An Introduction to Rigging in the Entertainment Industry and Rigging for Entertainment: Regulations and Practice, has collected together 50 articles he has provided regularly for Lighting + Sound International magazine from 2005 to date. They provide a wealth of information for those practising the craft within the entertainment technology industry. The book is profusely illustrated with caricature drawings by Christiano Giavedoni, featuring the popular rigging expert Mario.

ABC of Theatre Jargon *Francis Reid 106pp* **£9.95**   ISBN: 9781904031093
This glossary of theatrical terminology explains the common words and phrases that are used in normal conversation between actors, directors, designers, technicians and managers.

Aluminium Structures in the Entertainment Industry *Peter Hind 234pp* **£24.95**
ISBN: 9781904031062
Aluminium Structures in the Entertainment Industry aims to educate the reader in all aspects of the design and safe usage of temporary and permanent aluminium structures specific to the entertainment industry – such as roof structures, PA towers, temporary staging, etc.

AutoCAD – A Handbook for Theatre Users *David Ripley 340pp* **£29.95**
ISBN: 9781904031741
From 'Setting Up' to 'Drawing in Three Dimensions' via 'Drawings Within Drawings', this compact and fully illustrated guide to AutoCAD covers everything from the basics to full colour rendering and remote 3D plotting. Third, completely revised edition, June 2014.

Automation in the Entertainment Industry – A User's Guide *Mark Ager and John Hastie 382pp* **£29.95**   ISBN: 9781904031581
In the last 15 years, there has been a massive growth in the use of automation in entertainment, especially in theatres, and it is now recognised as its own discipline. However, it is still only used in around 5% of theatres worldwide. In the next 25 years, given current growth patterns, that figure will rise to 30%. This will mean that the majority of theatre personnel, including directors, designers, technical staff, actors and theatre management, will come into contact with automation for the first time at some point in their careers. This book is intended to provide insights and practical advice from those who use automation, to help the first-time user understand the issues and avoid the pitfalls in its implementation.

Basics – A Beginner's Guide to Lighting Design *Peter Coleman 92pp* **£9.95**
ISBN: 9781904031413
The fourth in the author's 'Basics' series, this title covers the subject area in four main sections: The Concept, Practical Matters, Related Issues and The Design Into Practice. In an

area that is difficult to be definitive, there are several things that cross all the boundaries of all lighting design and it's these areas that the author seeks to help with.

Basics – A Beginner's Guide to Special Effects *Peter Coleman 82pp* **£9.95**
ISBN: 9781904031338
This title introduces newcomers to the world of special effects. It describes all types of special effects including pyrotechnic, smoke and lighting effects, projections, noise machines, etc. It places emphasis on the safe storage, handling and use of pyrotechnics.

Basics – A Beginner's Guide to Stage Lighting *Peter Coleman 86pp* **£9.95**
ISBN: 9781904031208
This title does what it says: it introduces newcomers to the world of stage lighting. It will not teach the reader the art of lighting design, but will teach beginners much about the 'nuts and bolts' of stage lighting.

Basics – A Beginner's Guide to Stage Sound *Peter Coleman 86pp* **£9.95**
ISBN: 9781904031277
This title does what it says: it introduces newcomers to the world of stage sound. It will not teach the reader the art of sound design, but will teach beginners much about the background to sound reproduction in a theatrical environment.

Basics: A Beginner's Guide to Stage Management *Peter Coleman 64pp* **£7.95**
ISBN: 9781904031475
The fifth in Peter Coleman's popular 'Basics' series, this title provides a practical insight into, and the definition of, the role of stage management. Further chapters describe Cueing or 'Calling' the Show (the Prompt Book), and the Hardware and Training for Stage Management. This is a book about people and systems, without which most of the technical equipment used by others in the performance workplace couldn't function.

Building Better Theaters *Michael Mell 180pp* **£16.95** ISBN: 9781904031406
A title within our Consultancy Series, this book describes the process of designing a theatre, from the initial decision to build through to opening night. Michael Mell's book provides a step-by-step guide to the design and construction of performing arts facilities. Chapters discuss: assembling your team, selecting an architect, different construction methods, the architectural design process, construction of the theatre, theatrical systems and equipment, the stage, backstage, the auditorium, ADA requirements and the lobby. Each chapter clearly describes what to expect and how to avoid surprises. It is a must-read for architects, planners, performing arts groups, educators and anyone who may be considering building or renovating a theatre.

Carry on Fading *Francis Reid 216pp* **£20.00** ISBN: 9781904031642
This is a record of five of the best years of the author's life. Years so good that the only downside is the pangs of guilt at enjoying such contentment in a world full of misery induced by greed, envy and imposed ideologies. Fortunately Francis' DNA is high on luck, optimism and blessing counting.

Case Studies in Crowd Management
Chris Kemp, Iain Hill, Mick Upton, Mark Hamilton 206pp **£16.95**
ISBN: 9781904031482
This important work has been compiled from a series of research projects carried out by
the staff of the Centre for Crowd Management and Security Studies at Buckinghamshire
Chilterns University College (now Bucks New University), and seminar work carried out
in Berlin and Groningen with partner Yourope. It includes case studies, reports and a crowd
management safety plan for a major outdoor rock concert, safe management of rock concerts
utilising a triple barrier safety system and pan-European Health & Safety Issues.

Case Studies in Crowd Management, Security and Business Continuity
Chris Kemp, Patrick Smith 274pp **£24.95** ISBN: 9781904031635
The creation of good case studies to support work in progress and to give answers to those
seeking guidance in their quest to come to terms with perennial questions is no easy task.
The first Case Studies in Crowd Management book focused mainly on a series of festivals
and events that had a number of issues which required solving. This book focuses on a
series of events that had major issues that impacted on the every day delivery of the events
researched.

Close Protection – The Softer Skills *Geoffrey Padgham 132pp* **£11.95**
ISBN: 9781904031390
This is the first educational book in a new 'Security Series' for Entertainment
Technology Press, and it coincides with the launch of the new 'Protective Security
Management' Foundation Degree at Buckinghamshire Chilterns University College
(now Bucks New University). The author is a former full-career Metropolitan Police
Inspector from New Scotland Yard with 27 years' experience of close protection (CP).
For 22 of those years he specialised in operations and senior management duties with
the Royalty Protection Department at Buckingham Palace, followed by five years
in the private security industry specialising in CP training design and delivery. His
wealth of protection experience comes across throughout the text, which incorporates
sound advice and exceptional practical guidance, subtly separating fact from fiction.
This publication is an excellent form of reference material for experienced operatives,
students and trainees.

A Comparative Study of Crowd Behaviour at Two Major Music Events
Chris Kemp, Iain Hill, Mick Upton 78pp **£7.95** ISBN: 9781904031253
A compilation of the findings of reports made at two major live music concerts, and in
particular crowd behaviour, which is followed from ingress to egress.

Control Freak *Wayne Howell 270pp* **£28.95** ISBN: 9781904031550
Control Freak is the second book by Wayne Howell. It provides an in depth study of
DMX512 and the new RDM (Remote Device Management) standards. The book is aimed
at both users and developers and provides a wealth of real world information based on the
author's twenty year experience of lighting control.

Copenhagen Opera House *Richard Brett and John Offord 272pp* **£32.00**
ISBN: 9781904031420
Completed in a little over three years, the Copenhagen Opera House opened with a royal
gala performance on 15th January 2005. Built on a spacious brown-field site, the building
is a landmark venue and this book provides the complete technical background story
to an opera house set to become a benchmark for future design and planning. Sixteen
chapters by relevant experts involved with the project cover everything from the planning
of the auditorium and studio stage, the stage engineering, stage lighting and control and
architectural lighting through to acoustic design and sound technology plus technical
summaries.

Cue 80 *Francis Reid 310pp* **£17.95** ISBN: 9781904031659
Although Francis Reid's work in theatre has been visual rather than verbal, writing has
provided crucial support. Putting words on paper has been the way in which he organised
and clarified his thoughts. And in his self-confessed absence of drawing skills, writing has
helped him find words to communicate his visual thinking in discussions with the rest of
the creative team. As a by-product, this process of searching for the right words to help
formulate and analyse ideas has resulted in half-a-century of articles in theatre journals.
Cue 80 is an anthology of these articles and is released in celebration of Francis' 80th
birthday.

**The DMX 512-A Handbook – Design and Implementation of DMX Enabled Products
and Networks** *James Eade 150pp* **£13.95** ISBN: 9781904031727
This guidebook was originally conceived as a guide to the new DMX512-A standard on
behalf of the ESTA Controls Protocols Working Group (CPWG). It has subsequently been
updated and is aimed at all levels of reader from technicians working with or servicing
equipment in the field as well as manufacturers looking to build in DMX control to their
lighting products. It also gives thorough guidance to consultants and designers looking to
design DMX networks.

Electric Shadows: an Introduction to Video and Projection on Stage *Nick Moran 234pp*
£23.95 ISBN: 9781904031734
Electric Shadows aims to guide the emerging video designer through the many simple and
difficult technical and aesthetic choices and decisions he or she has to make in taking their
design from outline idea through to realisation. The main body of the book takes the reader
through the process of deciding what content will be projected onto what screen or screens
to make the best overall production design. The book will help you make electric shadows
that capture the attention of your audience, to help you tell your stories in just the way you
want.

Electrical Safety for Live Events *Marco van Beek 98pp* **£16.95** ISBN: 9781904031284
This title covers electrical safety regulations and good practise pertinent to the entertainment
industries and includes some basic electrical theory as well as clarifying the "do's and
don't's" of working with electricity.

Entertainment in Production Volume 1: 1994-1999 *Rob Halliday 254pp* **£24.95**
ISBN: 9781904031512

Entertainment in Production Volume 2: 2000-2006 *Rob Halliday 242poo* £24.95
ISBN: 9781904031529
Rob Halliday has a dual career as a lighting designer/programmer and author and in these
two volumes he provides the intriguing but comprehensive technical background stories
behind the major musical productions and other notable projects spanning the period 1994
to 2005. Having been closely involved with the majority of the events described, the author
is able to present a first-hand and all-encompassing portrayal of how many of the major
shows across the past decade came into being. From *Oliver!* and *Miss Saigon* to *Mamma
Mia!* and *Mary Poppins*, here the complete technical story unfolds. The books, which are
profusely illustrated, are in large part an adapted selection of articles that first appeared in
the magazine *Lighting&Sound International*.

Entertainment Technology Yearbook 2008 *John Offord 220pp* **£14.95**
ISBN: 9781904031543
The Entertainment Technology Yearbook 2008 covers the year 2007 and includes picture
coverage of major industry exhibitions in Europe compiled from the pages of Entertainment
Technology magazine and the etnow.com website, plus articles and pictures of production,
equipment and project highlights of the year.

The Exeter Theatre Fire *David Anderson 202pp* **£24.95** ISBN: 9781904031130
This title is a fascinating insight into the events that led up to the disaster at the Theatre
Royal, Exeter, on the night of September 5th 1887. The book details what went wrong, and
the lessons that were learned from the event.

Fading into Retirement *Francis Reid 124pp* **£17.95**
ISBN: 9781904031352
This is the final book in Francis Reid's fading trilogy which, with Fading Light and Carry
on Fading, updates the Hearing the Light record of places visited, performances seen,
and people met. Never say never, but the author uses the 'final' label because decreasing
mobility means that his ability to travel is diminished to the point that his life is now
contained within a very few square miles. His memories are triggered by over 600 CDs, half
of them Handel and 100 or so DVDs supplemented by a rental subscription to LOVEFiLM.

Fading Light – A Year in Retirement *Francis Reid 136pp* **£14.95**
ISBN: 9781904031352
Francis Reid, the lighting industry's favourite author, describes a full year in retirement.
"Old age is much more fun than I expected," he says. Fading Light describes visits and
experiences to the author's favourite theatres and opera houses, places of relaxation and re-
visits to scholarly institutions.

Focus on Lighting Technology *Richard Cadena 120pp* **£17.95** ISBN: 9781904031147
This concise work unravels the mechanics behind modern performance lighting and appeals

to designers and technicians alike. Packed with clear, easy-to-read diagrams, the book provides excellent explanations behind the technology of performance lighting.

The Followspot Guide *Nick Mobsby 450pp* **£28.95** ISBN: 9781904031499
The first in ETP's Equipment Series, Nick Mobsby's Followspot Guide tells you everything you need to know about followspots, from their history through to maintenance and usage. Its pages include a technical specification of 193 followspots from historical to the latest versions from major manufacturers.

From Ancient Rome to Rock 'n' Roll – a Review of the UK Leisure Security Industry
Mick Upton 198pp **£14.95** ISBN: 9781904031505
From stewarding, close protection and crowd management through to his engagement as a senior consultant Mick Upton has been ever present in the events industry. A founder of ShowSec International in 1982 he was its chairman until 2000. The author has led the way on training within the sector. He set up the ShowSec Training Centre and has acted as a consultant at the Bramshill Police College. He has been prominent in the development of courses at Buckinghamshire New University where he was awarded a Doctorate in 2005. Mick has received numerous industry awards. His book is a personal account of the development and professionalism of the sector across the past 50 years.

Gobos for Image Projection *Michael Hall and Julie Harper 176pp* **£25.95**
ISBN: 9781904031628
In this first published book dedicated totally to the gobo, the authors take the reader through from the history of projection to the development of the present day gobo. And there is broad practical advice and ample reference information to back it up. A feature of the work is the inclusion, interspersed throughout the text, of comment and personal experience in the use and application of gobos from over 25 leading lighting designers worldwide.

Health and Safety Aspects in the Live Music Industry *Chris Kemp, Iain Hill 300pp*
£30.00 ISBN: 9781904031222
This major work includes chapters on various safety aspects of live event production and is written by specialists in their particular areas of expertise.

Health and Safety in the Live Music and Event Technical Produciton Industry
Chris Hannam 74pp **£12.95** ISBN: 9781904031802
This book covers the real basics of health and safety in the live music and event production industry in a simple jargon free manner that can also be used as the perfect student course note accompaniment to the various safety passport schemes that now exist in our industry.

Health and Safety Management in the Live Music and Events Industry *Chris Hannam*
480pp **£25.95** ISBN: 9781904031307
This title covers the health and safety regulations and their application regarding all aspects of staging live entertainment events, and is an invaluable manual for production managers and event organisers.

Hearing the Light – 50 Years Backstage *Francis Reid 280pp* **£24.95**
ISBN: 9781904031185
This highly enjoyable memoir delves deeply into the theatricality of the industry. The author's almost fanatical interest in opera, his formative period as lighting designer at Glyndebourne and his experiences as a theatre administrator, writer and teacher make for a broad and unique background.

Introduction to Live Sound *Roland Higham 174pp* **£16.95**
ISBN: 9781904031796
This new title aims to provide working engineers and newcomers alike with a concise knowledge base that explains some of the theory and principles that they will encounter every day. It should provide for the student and newcomer to the field a valuable compendium of helpful knowledge.

An Introduction to Rigging in the Entertainment Industry *Chris Higgs 272pp* **£24.95**
ISBN: 9781904031123
This title is a practical guide to rigging techniques and practices and also thoroughly covers safety issues and discusses the implications of working within recommended guidelines and regulations. Second edition revised September 2008.

Let There be Light – Entertainment Lighting Software Pioneers in Conversation
Robert Bell 390pp **£32.00** ISBN: 9781904031246
Robert Bell interviews a distinguished group of software engineers working on entertainment lighting ideas and products.

Light and Colour Filters *Michael Hall and Eddie Ruffell 286pp* **£23.95**
ISBN: 9781904031598
Written by two acknowledged and respected experts in the field, this book is destined to become the standard reference work on the subject. The title chronicles the development and use of colour filters and also describes how colour is perceived and how filters function. Up-to-date reference tables will help the practitioner make better and more specific choices of colour.

Lighting for Roméo and Juliette *John Offord 172pp* **£26.95** ISBN: 9781904031161
John Offord describes the making of the Vienna State Opera production from the lighting designer's viewpoint – from the point where director Jürgen Flimm made his decision not to use scenery or sets and simply employ the expertise of lighting designer Patrick Woodroffe.

Lighting Systems for TV Studios *Nick Mobsby 570pp* **£45.00** ISBN: 9781904031000
Lighting Systems for TV Studios, now in its second edition, is the first book specifically written on the subject and has become the 'standard' resource work for studio planning and design covering the key elements of system design, luminaires, dimming, control, data networks and suspension systems as well as detailing the infrastructure items such as cyclorama, electrical and ventilation. TV lighting principles are explained and some history on TV broadcasting, camera technology and the equipment is provided to help set the scene!

The second edition includes applications for sine wave and distributed dimming, moving lights, Ethernet and new cool lamp technology.

Lighting Techniques for Theatre-in-the-Round   *Jackie Staines 188pp*   **£24.95**
ISBN: 9781904031017
Lighting Techniques for Theatre-in-the-Round is a unique reference source for those working on lighting design for theatre-in-the-round for the first time. It is the first title to be published specifically on the subject and it also provides some anecdotes and ideas for more challenging shows, and attempts to blow away some of the myths surrounding lighting in this format.

Lighting the Diamond Jubilee Concert   *Durham Marenghi 102pp*   **£19.95**
ISBN: 9781904031673
In this highly personal landmark document the show's lighting designer Durham Marenghi pays tribute to the team of industry experts who each played an important role in bringing the Diamond Jubilee Concert to fruition, both for television and live audiences. The book contains colour production photography throughout and describes the production processes and the thinking behind them. In his Foreword, BBC Executive Producer Guy Freeman states: "Working with the whole lighting team on such a special project was a real treat for me and a fantastic achievement for them, which the pages of this book give a remarkable insight into."

Lighting the Stage   *Francis Reid 120pp*   **£14.95**   ISBN: 9781904031086
Lighting the Stage discusses the human relationships involved in lighting design – both between people, and between these people and technology. The book is written from a highly personal viewpoint and its 'thinking aloud' approach is one that Francis Reid has used in his writings over the past 30 years.

Miscellany of Lighting and Stagecraft   *Michael Hall & Julie Harper 222pp*   **£22.95**
ISBN: 9781904031680
This title will help schools, colleges, amateurs, technicians and all those interested in practical theatre and performance to understand, in an entertaining and informative way, the key backstage skills. Within its pages, numerous professionals share their own special knowledge and expertise, interspersed with diversions of historic interest and anecdotes from those practising at the front line of the industry. As a result, much of the advice and skills set out have not previously been set in print. The editors' intention with this book is to provide a Miscellany that is not ordered or categorised in strict fashion, but rather encourages the reader to flick through or dip into it, finding nuggets of information and anecdotes to entertain, inspire and engender curiosity – also to invite further research or exploration and generally encourage people to enter the industry and find out for themselves.

Mr Phipps' Theatre   *Mark Jones, John Pick 172pp*   £17.95   ISBN: 9781904031383
Mark Jones and John Pick describe "The Sensational Story of Eastbourne's Royal Hippodrome" – formerly Eastbourne Theatre Royal. An intriguing narrative, the book sets the story against a unique social history of the town. Peter Longman, former director of The Theatres Trust, provides the Foreword.

Northen Lights *Michael Northen 256pp* **£17.95** ISBN: 9781904031666
Many books have been written by famous personalities in the theatre about their lives and work. However this is probably one of the first memoirs by someone who has spent his entire career behind scenes, and not in front of the footlights. As a lighting designer and as consultant to designers and directors, Michael Northen worked through an exciting period of fifty years of theatrical history from the late nineteen thirties in theatres in the UK and abroad, and on productions ranging from Shakespeare, opera and ballet to straight plays, pantomimes and cabaret. This is not a complicated technical text book, but is intended to give an insight into some of the 300 productions in which he had been involved and some of the directors, the designers and backstage staff he have worked with, viewed from a new angle.

Pages From Stages *Anthony Field 204pp* **£17.95** ISBN: 9781904031260
Anthony Field explores the changing style of theatres including interior design, exterior design, ticket and seat prices, and levels of service, while questioning whether the theatre still exists as a place of entertainment for regular theatre-goers.

People, Places, Performances *Remembered by Francis Reid 60pp* **£8.95**
ISBN: 9781904031765
In growing older, the Author has found that memories, rather than featuring the events, increasingly tend to focus on the people who caused them, the places where they happened and the performances that arose. So Francis Reid has used these categories in endeavouring to compile a brief history of the second half of the twentieth century.

Performing Arts Technical Training Handbook 2013/2014 *ed: John Offord 304pp*
£19.95 ISBN: 9781904031710
Published in association with the ABTT (Association of British Theatre Technicians), this important Handbook, now in its third edition, includes fully detailed and indexed entries describing courses on backstage crafts offered by over 100 universities and colleges across the UK. A completely new research project, with accompanying website, the title also includes articles with advice for those considering a career 'behind the scenes', together with contact information and descriptions of the major organisations involved with industry training – plus details of companies offering training within their own premises.

Practical Dimming *Nick Mobsby 364pp* **£22.95** ISBN: 97819040313444
This important and easy to read title covers the history of electrical and electronic dimming, how dimmers work, current dimmer types from around the world, planning of a dimming system, looking at new sine wave dimming technology and distributed dimming. Integration of dimming into different performance venues as well as the necessary supporting electrical systems are fully detailed. Significant levels of information are provided on the many different forms and costs of potential solutions as well as how to plan specific solutions. Architectural dimming for the likes of hotels, museums and shopping centres is included. Practical Dimming is a companion book to Practical DMX and is designed for all involved in the use, operation and design of dimming systems.

Practical DMX *Nick Mobsby 276pp* **£16.95** ISBN: 9781904031369
In this highly topical and important title the author details the principles of DMX, how to plan a network, how to choose equipment and cables, with data on products from around the world, and how to install DMX networks for shows and on a permanently installed basis. The easy style of the book and the helpful fault finding tips, together with a review of different DMX testing devices provide an ideal companion for all lighting technicians and system designers. An introduction to Ethernet and Canbus networks are provided as well as tips on analogue networks and protocol conversion. It also includes a chapter on Remote Device Management.

A Practical Guide to Health and Safety in the Entertainment Industry
Marco van Beek 120pp **£14.95** ISBN: 9781904031048
This book is designed to provide a practical approach to Health and Safety within the Live Entertainment and Event industry. It gives industry-pertinent examples, and seeks to break down the myths surrounding Health and Safety.

Production Management *Joe Aveline 134pp* **£17.95** ISBN: 9781904031109
Joe Aveline's book is an in-depth guide to the role of the Production Manager, and includes real-life practical examples and 'Aveline's Fables' – anecdotes of his experiences with real messages behind them.

Rigging for Entertainment: Regulations and Practice *Chris Higgs 156pp* **£19.95**
ISBN: 9781904031215
Continuing where he left off with his highly successful An Introduction to Rigging in the Entertainment Industry, Chris Higgs' second title covers the regulations and use of equipment in greater detail.

Rock Solid Ethernet *Wayne Howell 304pp* **£23.95** ISBN: 9781904031697
Now in its third completely revised and reset edition, Rock Solid Ethernet is aimed specifically at specifiers, installers and users of entertainment industry systems, and will give the reader a thorough grounding in all aspects of computer networks, whatever industry they may work in. The inclusion of historical and technical 'sidebars' make for an enjoyable as well as an informative read.

Sixty Years of Light Work *Fred Bentham 450pp* **£26.95** ISBN: 9781904031079
This title is an autobiography of one of the great names behind the development of modern stage lighting equipment and techniques. It includes a complete facsimile of the famous Strand Electric Catalogue of May 1936 – a reference work in itself.

Sound for the Stage *Patrick Finelli 218pp* **£24.95** ISBN: 9781904031154
Patrick Finelli's thorough manual covering all aspects of live and recorded sound for performance is a complete training course for anyone interested in working in the field of stage sound, and is a must for any student of sound.

Stage Automation *Anton Woodward 128pp* **£12.95** ISBN: 9781904031567
The purpose of this book is to explain the stage automation techniques used in modern theatre to achieve some of the spectacular visual effects seen in recent years. The book is targeted at automation operators, production managers, theatre technicians, stage engineering machinery manufacturers and theatre engineering students. Topics are covered in sufficient detail to provide an insight into the thought processes that the stage automation engineer has to consider when designing a control system to control stage machinery in a modern theatre. The author has worked on many stage automation projects and developed the award-winning Impressario stage automation system.

Stage Lighting Design in Britain: The Emergence of the Lighting Designer, 1881-1950
Nigel Morgan 300pp **£17.95** ISBN: 9781904031345
This title sets out to ascertain the main course of events and the controlling factors that determined the emergence of the theatre lighting designer in Britain, starting with the introduction of incandescent electric light to the stage, and ending at the time of the first public lighting design credits around 1950. The book explores the practitioners, equipment, installations and techniques of lighting design.

Stage Lighting for Theatre Designers *Nigel Morgan 124pp* **£17.95**
ISBN: 9781904031192
This is an updated second edition of Nigel Morgan's popular book for students of theatre design – outlining all the techniques of stage lighting design.

Technical Marketing Techniques *David Brooks, Andy Collier, Steve Norman 160pp*
£24.95 ISBN: 9781904031031
Technical Marketing is a novel concept, defined and elaborated by the authors of this book, with business-to-business companies competing in fast developing technical product sectors.

Technical Standards for Places of Entertainment *ABTT 354pp A4* **£45.00**
ISBN: 9781904031703
Technical Standards for Places of Entertainment details the necessary physical standards required for entertainment venues. Known in the industry as the "Yellow Book" the latest completely revised edition was first published in June 2013.

Theatre Engineering and Stage Machinery *Toshiro Ogawa 332pp* **£30.00**
ISBN: 9781904031024
Theatre Engineering and Stage Machinery is a unique reference work covering every aspect of theatrical machinery and stage technology in global terms, and across the complete historical spectrum. Revised February 2007.

Theatre Lighting in the Age of Gas *Terence Rees 232pp* **£24.95**
ISBN: 9781904031178
Entertainment Technology Press has republished this valuable historic work previously produced by the Society for Theatre Research in 1978. Theatre Lighting in the Age of Gas investigates the technological and artistic achievements of theatre lighting engineers from the 1700s to the late Victorian period.

Theatre Space: A Rediscovery Reported *Francis Reid 238pp* **£19.95**
ISBN: 9781904031437
In the post-war world of the 1950s and 60s, the format of theatre space became a matter for
a debate that aroused passions of an intensity unknown before or since. The proscenium
arch was clearly identified as the enemy, accused of forming a barrier to disrupt the relations
between the actor and audience. An uneasy fellow-traveller at the time, Francis Reid later
recorded his impressions whilst enjoying performances or working in theatres old and new
and this book is an important collection of his writings in various theatrical journals from
1969-2001 including his contribution to the Cambridge Guide to the Theatre in 1988. It
reports some of the flavour of the period when theatre architecture was rediscovering its past
in a search to establish its future.

The Theatres and Concert Halls of Fellner and Helmer *Michael Sell 246pp* **£23.95**
ISBN: 9781904031772
This is the first British study of the works of the prolific Fellner and Helmer Atelier which
was active from 1871-1914 during which time they produced over 80 theatre designs and are
second in quantity only to Frank Matcham, to whom reference is made.
This period is one of great change as a number of serious theatre fires which included Nice
and Vienna had the effect of the introduction of safety legislation which affected theatre
design. This study seeks to show how Fellner and Helmer and Frank Matcham dealt with
this increasing safety legislation, in particular the way in which safety was built into their
new three part theatres equipped with iron stages, safety curtains, electricity and appropriate
access and egress and, in the Vienna practice, how this was achieved across 13 countries.

Theatres of Achievement *John Higgins 302pp* **£29.95** ISBN: 9781904031376
John Higgins affectionately describes the history of 40 distinguished UK theatres in a
personal tribute, each uniquely illustrated by the author. Completing each profile is colour
photography by Adrian Eggleston.

Theatric Tourist *Francis Reid 220pp* **£19.95** ISBN: 9781904031468
Theatric Tourist is the delightful story of Francis Reid's visits across more than 50 years
to theatres, theatre museums, performances and even movie theme parks. In his inimitable
style, the author involves the reader within a personal experience of venues from the Legacy
of Rome to theatres of the Renaissance and Eighteenth Century Baroque and the Gustavian
Theatres of Stockholm. His performance experiences include Wagner in Beyreuth, the
Pleasures of Tivoli and Wayang in Singapore. This is a 'must have' title for those who are as
"incurably stagestruck" as the author.

Through the Viewfinder *Jeremy Hoare 276pp* **£21.95** ISBN:: 9781904031574
Do you want to be a top television cameraman? Well this is going to help!
Through the Viewfinder is aimed at media students wanting to be top professional television
cameramen – but it will also be of interest to anyone who wants to know what goes on
behind the cameras that bring so much into our homes.
The author takes his own opinionated look at how to operate a television camera based on
23 years' experience looking through many viewfinders for a major ITV network company.

Based on interviews with people he has worked with, all leaders in the profession, the book is based on their views and opinions and is a highly revealing portrait of what happens behind the scenes in television production from a cameraman's point of view.

Walt Disney Concert Hall – The Backstage Story *Patricia MacKay & Richard Pilbrow*
250pp **£28.95** ISBN: 9781904031239
Spanning the 16-year history of the design and construction of the Walt Disney Concert Hall, this book provides a fresh and detailed behind the scenes story of the design and technology from a variety of viewpoints. This is the first book to reveal the "process" of the design of a concert hall.

Yesterday's Lights – A Revolution Reported *Francis Reid 352pp* **£26.95**
ISBN: 9781904031321
Set to help new generations to be aware of where the art and science of theatre lighting is coming from – and stimulate a nostalgia trip for those who lived through the period, Francis Reid's latest book has over 350 pages dedicated to the task, covering the 'revolution' from the fifties through to the present day. Although this is a highly personal account of the development of lighting design and technology and he admits that there are 'gaps', you'd be hard put to find anything of significance missing.

Go to www.etbooks.co.uk for full details of above titles and secure online ordering facilities. Most books also available for Kindle.